Jujutsu, Sword & Spear

柔術と撃剣

A Guide to Self-Defense · Published 1906

Hisamatsu Sadamoto

Translated by Eric Shahan

Translator's Introduction

Jujutsu, Gekken & Spear: A Guide to Self-Defense was published in 1906. The author, Hisamatsu Sadamoto, previously wrote three other books on martial arts in 1898, under the name Sugawara Sadamoto. They were *Gekken*, *Jujutsu* and *Kenbu*. In this book, *Jujutsu, Gekken & Spear: A Guide to Self-Defense,* the author incudes both basic and advanced fighting techniques based on scenarios taken from his real-life experiences. The sections detailing how to deal with intruders in your house as well as techniques showing how to fight multiple opponents armed with a variety of weapons are unique to this book.

Jujutsu, Gekken & Spear: A Guide to Self-Defense was published with a few errors related to page numbers. For example, the second page of the table of contents is missing as is the first page of the introduction. Since the pages do not appear ripped out this is likely a printing error. Further, the illustrations for some techniques are out of order. In addition, some techniques from the same topic are mixed in with others. For example, a "standing technique," would appear in the middle of the section for "seated techniques." While I initially thought to translate the book "as is," in the end I elected to group all the techniques according to the original intent of the book, to give a coherent understanding of the techniques.

While the author digresses frequently, and some steps receive vastly more explanation than others, he states the techniques are based on his own experiences or that of his acquaintances. The techniques are generally explained twice, once for an overview and then again with a more detailed explanation of each illustration. Unfortunately, there is no additional information about Hisamatsu Sadamoto.

Jujutsu to Gekken Mokuroku

柔術と撃劔

Catalogue of Jujutsu and Gekken Techniques

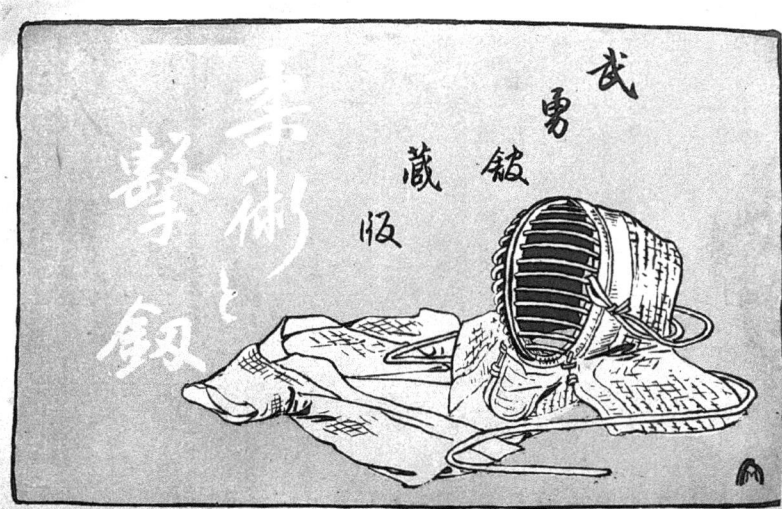

Jujutsu to Gekken Mokuroku
Catalogue of Jujutsu and Gekken Techniques
Table of Contents

Jujutsu to Gekken Mokuroku
Catalogue of Jujutsu and Gekken Techniques
Using Jujutsu Against One Opponent and Three Opponents

- Jujutsu is the Mother and Father of the Six Martial Arts[1]
- Authenticity in Jujutsu
- A Person with Jujutsu Training Can Escape from Unexpected Danger
- Jujutsu is a Shapeless Self-Protection Device
- If You Train in Jujutsu and Gekken, It Will be Good Exercise and Make You Healthier
- First Lesson In Jujutsu
- List of Places To Grab
- List of Places to Hit
- List of Places to Pierce
- List of Places to Kick
- List of Places to Strike With the Knee
- List of Places to Wrap Up
- List of Common Jujutsu Terms
- How to Defend Vulnerable Parts of Your Body
- Regarding the Keikogi
- How to Bow When Doing a Seated Technique
  Illustrations 1 ~ 3
- Seated Technique: Rolling Over the Right Elbow
  Illustrations 1 ~ 6
- Seated Technique: Pulling and Rolling Over
  Illustrations 1 ~ 2
- How to Bow When Doing a Standing Techniques
- Standing Technique: Crossing Paths on the Left
  Illustrations 1 ~ 3

---

[1] This page is missing from the book.

Authenticity in Jujutsu

二　　　　　　　　柔　　　　　　　術

妙に通ずるを謂ふて可なり。

○柔術に眞僞ある事

柔術なるものは、力の劣る者、己の力に勝る剛力の者に遭ふとも、其剛敵の力を柔かに受け、柔を以て敵の力を利用し、而して勝を取るの術なり、即ち敵は己の力にて己が投られ、或は伏せらるゝなり、此書に示す諸形を見れば、自ら術の妙、即ち力の劣れる者も、力の勝れる者に勝つの理を知るを得べし、例へば十七八歳の處女も壮士を投げ伏するの不思議ならぬを覺り得べし、夫の小説本などに武者修行する者が、幾人も敵しては投げ、執ては伏せるゝ書けるなり、強ち其武士に怪力あらうに非ず、實は此術に長けたるなり、是等を眞の柔術とす、然るに之を誤りて、柔術なりと稱へながら、術と云ふものは更に無くして、力づくにて取合ひ勝負を決する流儀あり、是等は僞りと謂ふ可きなり、斯の如くならば、力の強き者は、必ず力の弱き者に勝ち、力の弱き

Escaping From Unexpected Danger Without Jujutsu

三　　　　　　　　柔　　　　　　　術

者は、必ず力の強き者に負くることにて術ごとは謂ふべからず、斯るものは徒に力競べにて、相撲に似たるものなり、撲相にすら四十八手ありと聞く、されば少しは術あるべし、然るに柔術と云ひて徒に力くらべするは、此相撲にだも如かずと謂ふて可ならむ、柔術は主として、柔の字に眼を著くべし、剛になりては誤りなり、此眞術を誤りたる者は、決して術にはあらねど、假に剛術と名づけて、眞傳を守る者は笑ふなり、本書を見て、能々此差別を識るべし。

○柔術の心得ある者は不意の危難を免るゝを得る事

柔術を心得たる者は、不意に多勢に襲はれ、止むを得ずして逃るゝ時、諸の障害物を飛越え、又は竹木に登り、竹などの挑め得らるゝ物は、其末を執りて、河沼も越ゆることを得るものなり、敵と勝負を決する時のみならず。

○柔術は無形の護身器なる事

Jujutsu is a Shapeless Self-Protection Device

四　　　　　　柔　　　　　　術

柔術を除くの外、凡そ敵を拒ぎて我身を
護るには凶器を携帯せざるを得ず、昔な
らば槍、薙刀、弓、劔、太刀、刀、脇差、匕
首、手裏劔、大砲、銃、執れか用ゐる
ざるを得ず、今は洋劔、砲、銃、短銃、
仕込杖等を用ゐれど、凶器を携たずして
敵を防ぐには、此柔術に限るなり、而して
洋劔、砲、銃を取扱ふは、夫々の係り官
にて、平人は何をも携へず、仕込杖、或
は短銃を携つ者ありても、人各持つもの
に非ず、昔は平人にても旅行には、旅帯
さて脇差一本を帯したれども、今は無腰
なり、誠に便り無きものなり、萬一にも
途中にて危難に遭はんとするときは、何
を以て免るべきを得ん、其時こそは、此柔
術の心得ありて可なるものなり、倘又少
壯の人は、必ず兵役を勤めざるべからず
將た尚武の時節にもあれば、武藝を研き
て、心丈夫に爲し置くべき事なり。

○柔術撃劔の稽古をすれば善き運
動となりて衛生に互益ある事

Jujutsu & Gekken: Good Exercise Will Make You Healthier
&
First Lesson In Jujutsu

五　　　　　　術　　　　　　柔

常に胃病を患ふ者は、運動の足らざる故
なり、之を免れむが爲めにとて、遠度の
運動を爲すことは、誰も識りたる事にて
體操もあれど、此稽古も亦、運動には好
きものなり。

○柔術初手の事
柔術の取はじめは、先づ眉間を打ちか
るを、或は片手或は兩手にて、敵の胸な
る襟を取るか、又は後背より抱き着きて
襟を取るか、又は二の腕を取
るかなり、但し左右の両手にて襟を取る
ときには、右の手を上にし、左の手を下
にするなり、此他捕搦きとて、敵の刀を
奪はんには、必ず其柄を兩手にて取るな
り、是等の事を爲す前、兩手とも空手の
時、或は片手の空手の時には、必ず拇指
を內にして、拳を爲し居るべし、又初
め身構へる時には、足を外八文字に踏む
べし。

○取る所の要處
喉、胸、肩、肱、二の腕、腕首、

List of Places To Grab
List of Places to Hit
List of Places to Pierce
List of Places to Kick
List of Places to Attack
List of Places to Wrap Up
&
List of Common Jujutsu Terms

眉間
○打つ所の要處

喉、暈丸、
○突く所の要處

暈丸、
○蹴る所の要處

脇三校、暈丸、
○中てる所の要處

坐するときは膝、立てるときは足、取伏せ、引倒す前には必ず此心得ある
○繋くる所の要處

べし、

○柔術の通語
これは一試合の事を云ふ。
一本
これは技の勝れたる方の人なり。
使手
これは技の劣りたる方の人なり。
受手
此書の畫に白き襦袢、又は白き服を着たる人は使手にて、黒き襦袢、又は黒き服を着たる人は受手なり、受手を又
單に受とも云ふ。
此他、打つ、受る、取る、掛る、外す、

How to Defend Vulnerable Parts of Your Body
& Regarding the Keikogi

柔術學

切る、拂ふ、蹴込む、上る、引く、押ば、伏る、投る、投げ、中てる中等あり、

○危険の要處を防ぐ心得
右の取る所の要處は、何れも注意し居るは無論なれども、殊に暈丸は、圍ふと云ひて、空きたる手にて撫ひ居るを忘るべからず。
是等をも記憶し置くべし。

○稽古着の事
稗を穿かず稗
古襦袢に長き
猿股引を穿く
なり。

6

○ Authenticity in Jujutsu

Those interested in Jujutsu know that even if you are of inferior strength and encounter a very strong man, you will be able to softly receive that strong person's power and flexibly adapt it. You can use his own power to defeat him. This how Jujutsu techniques work. In other words, your opponent is thrown or pulled down by his own application of power. By studying the methods shown in this book, you will be able to refine your own technique. This is because you will understand the underlying principle of a person of inferior strength defeating a person of superior strength.

For example, you will understand that it is not at all out of the ordinary for a young girl of 17 or 18 years of age, to throw an adult man to the ground. As for what is described in the ubiquitous novels about Musha Shugyo, a pilgrimage taken by martial artists to develop their skill, will often contain a scene of a man battling several opponents at the same time. The man will be depicted slamming all his adversaries to the ground. This is not because he possessed some supernatural strength it was because he was adept at Jujutsu. This is true Jujutsu.

However, on the other hand, you will find martial art schools mistakenly calling the art they teach "Jujutsu" when in fact there are no actual Jujutsu techniques being used. Such schools are only focused on pitting strength against strength. The people in charge of such schools should rightfully be called charlatans. In such a school the stronger person will invariably defeat a weaker person, and a weaker person will invariably lose to a stronger person. Thus, those who train at such school are not using Jujutsu techniques.

They are doing is competing in "tests of strength" which basically describes Sumo wrestling. However, even Sumo wrestling contains the 48 Hands, or 48 Official Ways to Win a Sumo Match. Therefore, though Sumo duels are basically tests of strength, they does contain some techniques. Any art that claims to be Jujutsu but instead relies solely on power against power, is a thing that is even lower than Sumo.

To understand what makes up Jujutsu you should fix your eye on the first Kanji of that word, Ju 柔, meaning soft and flexible. This first Kanji should not be Go 剛, stiff and rigid with power. People who mistake the true meaning of this art are unable to truly use techniques so they change *Jujutsu*, the art of soft and flexible to *Gojutsu*, the art of rigid strength. Such practitioners are a source of amusement to those following the true teachings of this art. If you read this book carefully you will learn how to differentiate between the two.

○ A Person with Jujutsu Training Can Escape from Unexpected Danger

If you have Jujutsu training and are unexpectedly assaulted by multiple opponents, and you have no option other than to flee, you can leap or duck around obstacles. In addition, you can climb a tree or tall piece of bamboo, or even pick up a piece of bamboo or a long stick and use that to cross over a river or swampy area. So you do not always have to directly confront your opponents.

○ Jujutsu is a Shapeless Self-Protection Device

Martial arts other than Jujutsu require that you have a weapon in order to defend yourself against an enemy. Long ago weapons like the spear, halberd, Tachi (long sword,) Katana, Wakizashi (short sword,) Kaiken (knife,) Shuriken (throwing stars or blades,) bow, cannon, rifle and so on were used. Nowadays, the western saber, cannon, rifle, pistol and Shikomi-zue (sword concealed in a cane,) are used. However, only Jujutsu allows you to defend yourself against an enemy without a weapon.

For the most part the people using cannons, rifles and sabers are in the armed forces. Average people do not carry carry any weapon. That being said, while there may be some people that carry a sword-cane or a pistol, these people are the exception.

In the Edo Era average people used to carry a Kaiken, pocket dagger, with them as they travelled however nowadays this is rare. So most people go about unarmed, without anything to defend themselves. If you are confronted by a dangerous person, how would you defend yourself? The answer in these situations is to use your knowledge of Jujutsu. While not every boy will enter the military, considering how important martial spirit is during this time, it is important to study martial arts and strengthen your mind and body.

Jujutsu & Gekken: Good Exercise Will Make You Healthier

For those suffering from stomach ailments, part of the problem is a lack of physical activity. Most people are aware that the best remedy for this is an appropriate amount of exercise. While there are gymnastics programs that are helpful, training in Jujutsu is a good option.

◯ First Lesson In Jujutsu

When beginning Jujutsu you will first learn things like how to strike to Miken, between the eyes, or how to seize your opponent's collar, sometimes with one hand other times with both hands. You will be taught how to approach your opponent from behind and wrap your arms around him and grab his collar. You might also grab your opponent's wrist or upper arm.

However, when you are grabbing both sides of your opponent's collar, it is important to remember that your right hand should grab high and your left hand should grab low.

There is also Tsuka Sabaki, which is either grabbing and controlling an opponent's sword handle or defending against someone grabbing the handle of your sword. When attempting to steal your opponent's sword, you must always grab it with two hands.

Also, when one or both hands are Karate, or empty, always make a fist by tucking your thumb against your palm and wrapping your fingers around it.[2]

Your initial stance should be with your feet in Soto Hachi Monji, or facing outward like the bottom of the Kanji for eight, 八.

------

[2] This illustration is from *A New Judo Instructor's Guide* by Sugawara Sadamoto published in Taisho 15 (1926.) The text says,

This is Atemi no Ken, Fist for Striking Vital Points on the Body. As shown in the illustration, tucking your thumb inside your other fingers you can make a solid and powerful fist.

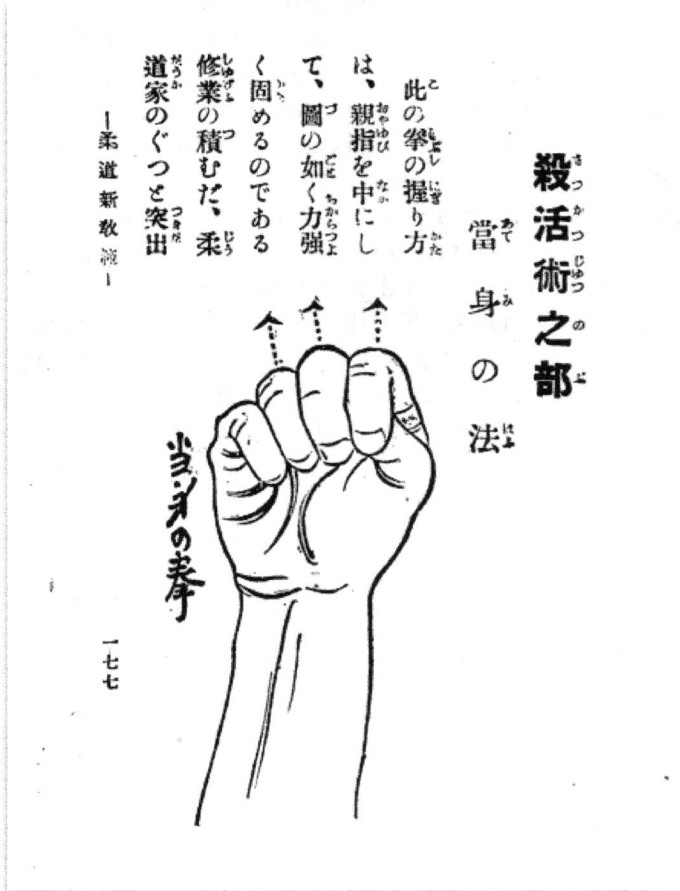

殺活術之部　當身の法

此の拳の握り方
は、親指を中にし
て、圖の如く力強
く固めるのである
修業の積むだ、柔
道家のぐつと突出

一柔道新教範一

当テ身ミの拳

一七七

○ **List of Places To Grab**

Nodo – Throat
Mune – Chest
Hiji – Elbow
Ninoude – Forearm or Upper Arm[3]
Udekubi – Elbow or Wrist[4]

○ **List of Places to Hit**

Miken – Between the Eyebrows

○ **List of Places to Pierce**

Nodo – Throat
Kinteki – Groin

○ **List of Places to Kick**

Kinteki – Groin

---

[3] Ninoude 二の腕 "Second part of the arm." The author uses this word to refer to both the forearm and the upper arm.
[4] Tekubi 手首- "Hand neck" is the most common word for wrist nowadays, however this book uses Udekubi 腕首, "Arm Neck." Based on the illustrations, the author sometimes uses this word to mean "elbow" and other times "wrist."

○ List of Places to Strike With the Knee

Abara Sanmai – Third Rib[5]
Kinteki – Groin

○ List of Places to Plant the Foot or Leg

When seated, you should plant your foot by your opponent's knee. When standing, plant your leg against your opponent's. Before you push or pull a person down, it is essential to be aware of this.

○ List of Common Jujutsu Terms

Ippon – This refers to one duel.
Tsukai-te – This refers to the person whose technique is superior.
Uke-te – This refers to the person whose technique is inferior.

In this document, the man wearing the white Juban, or shirt, and white Fuku, or pants, will be the Tsukai-te. Thus the person wearing the black clothing will be the Uke-te. The Uke-te will also be referred to simply as Uke.[6]

---

[5] Abara Sanmai 肋三枚 : Third rib. This is a Kyusho, vital point, that is kind of tricky to locate since each school of martial arts indicate it is in different place. The term originates from Mataki-words, or language used by hunters in northern Japan. It indicates the best spot to shoot (or stab with a spear) a bear. The reason is the heart is directly on the other side. On a human this would be the ribs below the armpit. However, some schools refer to this spot as where the floating ribs are located. Since these are not attached to the sternum, they are easier to break, and are considered a good place to strike for maximum damage.
[6] For simplicity, the two combatants will be "You" and "Attacker."

○ How to Defend Vulnerable Parts of Your Body

You should always exercise caution when grabbing your opponent, as was described previously. In particular, you should protect the area around your groin. Thus, do not forget to position your free hand around that area.

○ Regarding the Keikogi , or Training Uniform

A Hakama is not worn. Use a long Juban shirt as a Keikogi and wear Sarumata "monkey pants" below.

Translator's Note:

The author does not include a chart showing Kyuhso, vital striking points, so I have reproduced one from *How to Become Expert at Judo,* which was published in 1939 by the Judo Educational Research Society. This chart also shows how to strike with different parts of the body.

柔道上達法 *How to Become Expert at Judo*
柔道教育研究会 Judo Educational Research Society
Published1939
Illustration 1 : *Jintai no Kyusho to Atemi-waza wo Hodokosu Bubun*
Vital Points and Places to Strike on the Body

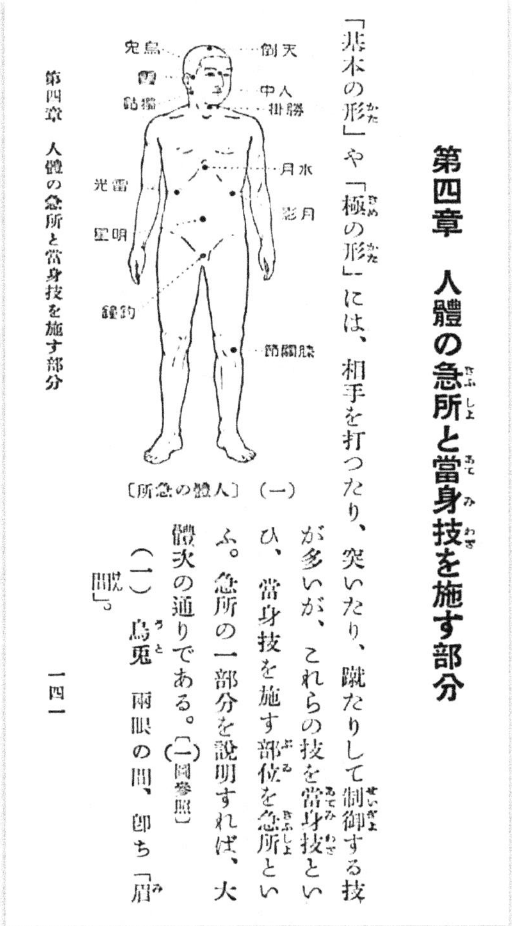

第四章　人體の急所と當身技を施す部分

「悲本の形」や「極の形」には、相手を打つたり、突いたり、蹴たりして制御する技が多いが、これらの技を當身技といひ、當身技を施す部位を急所といふ。急所の一部分を説明すれば、大體次の通りである。(一)圖參照

(一)烏兎　兩眼の間、即ち「眉間」。

〔所急の體人〕(一)

[Figure labels:]
第四章　人體の急所と當身技を施す部分

宛鳥
霞
結喉

創天
中人
扣膊

月水
影月

光雷
里明

鐘釣

節關膝

一四

In the Basic Forms and the Ultimate Forms there are many techniques where you are punching, striking and kicking in order to control your opponent. These are all known as Atemi Waza, or Striking Techniques. The points you are striking when doing these techniques are called Kyusho, Vital Points. The following is an explanation of these striking points. Please refer to the illustration.

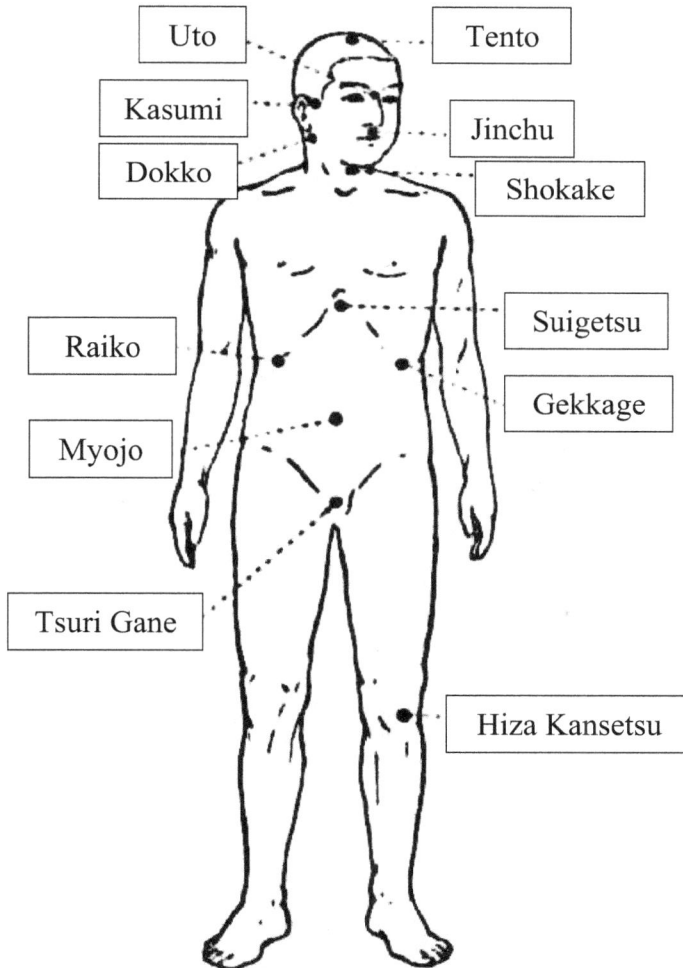

[所急の體人] (一)

Illustration 1: Vital Points on the Body

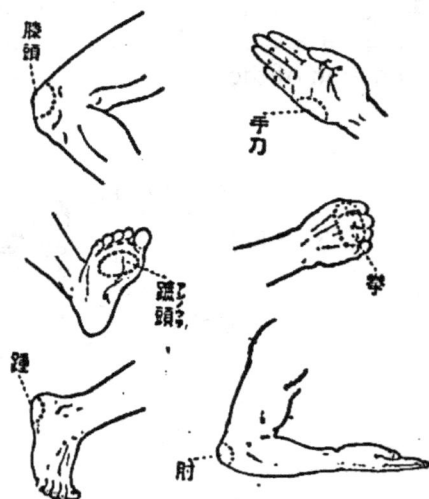

〔當身技を施す部分〕（二）

(二) 人中（じんちゅう）　鼻下中央部。

(三) 霞（かすみ）　いはゆる「こめかみ」

(四) 水月（すゐげつ）　いはゆる「みづおち」

(五) 電光・月影（でんくわう・げつえん）　右の季肋部（肋骨の最下位の邊）が電光、左が月影。

(六) 明星（みゃうじゃう）　臍の下約一寸の邊。

(七) 釣鐘（つりがね）　睾丸（かうぐわん）。

なほ當身技を施す部分としては、圖に示すやうに、手刀即ち掌の小指の側（二）の軟かな部分や、拳や、足指の附根の裏の軟かな部分や、肘・膝頭・踵などを用ひる。

當身術を施すには、次の二つの注意事項を守らねばならぬ。

(イ) 打つ・突く・蹴るなどの動作が、反動でやや元に返る位に、いはゆる冴えをつけて施すこと。

(ロ) 相手の體勢を崩しながら施すこと。

16

Vital Points and Places to Strike on the Body

1. *Uto* – The Kanji for this vital point are "Rabbit Crow" and it refers to the spot between the eyes. Also known as Miken, meaning "between the eyebrows."
2. *Jinchu* – "Center of Man" The spot below the nose.
3. *Kasumi* – "Mist" This spot is also known as Komekami, "Bee Valley" the temple.
4. *Suigetsu* – "Moon Reflected on Water" Also known as Mizuochi "Water Drop" the solar plexus.
5. Denko · Getsuen "Lightning Bolt · Shadow of the Moon" The lower ribs on the right side are Lightning Bolt. (The lowest point of the ribcage.) The left side is called Shadow of the Moon.
6. Myoujo – "Bright Star" A spot 3 centimeters below the navel.
7. Tsurigane – "Hanging Bell" Also known as Kogan, the testicles.

As Illustration 2 shows, strike these points with Tegatana, referring to the soft spot below the little finger, as well as the fist, the soft spot on the bottom of your foot where your toes meet the foot, the elbow, knee and heel.

When striking keep the following points in mind:

- When striking, stabbing or kicking be sure that the rebound of the strike brings you back to your original position. Your movement should be clear and dexterous.
- The power of your strike should break your opponent's balance.

Illustration 2

Jintai no Kyusho to Atemi-waza wo Hodokosu Bubun
Vital Points and Places to Strike on the Body

Hizagashira
Kneecap

膝頭

Te-gatana
Knife Hand

手刀

Ashinoko
Ball of the foot

蹠頭

Ken
Fist

拳

踵

肘

〔當身技を施す部分〕（二）

Kakato
Heel

Hiji
Elbow

居捕

Idori : Seated Techniques

● Idori: Seated Techniques
Reishiki : How to Bow
Illustration 1

七　　　　　捕　　坐　　術　　柔

此科は坐りて捕る故坐捕と云ふ、さて捕

其一科目なり如く、坐捕は

に列べ記せし目録あ、りて、

柔術にも科目體式

◎坐捕

◎稽古着の事

袴を穿かず稽古褳神に長き猿股引を穿くなり。

〇危險の要處を防ぐ心得右の取る所の要處は、何れも注意し居るは無論なれども、殊に睾丸は、圍ふさと云ひて、空きたる手にて捂ひ居るを忘るべからず。

切る、拂ふ、蹴込む、上る、引く、押ほす、投る、投げ、中てる中て等あり、是等をも記臆し置くべし。

（圖　一　第）

● How to Bow : Illustration 2

捕　　坐　　術　・　柔　　　　　八

文字に蹈みながら雙方より互ひに一禮し左の膝も立て時によりては、其初め、立ちて足を外八兩手は兩膝へ置きながら進み合ひ、又、り左の圖の如く、互ひに右の膝を立て其心持ありて油斷せず、されよ手の拇指を内へ屈めず、されと、なれば、

禮をするうちだ捕り合はず、時は未り、此合ふな膝に置きて見手を兩

一間ほど空け、居合腰に胡坐をかき、兩下の圖の如く、雙方の間を六尺、卽ち始めに禮を爲す、體を爲すには一其初る

（圖　二　第）

● **How to Bow : Illustration 3**

柔術坐捕　九

徐々と近よりて居合腰に胡坐をかくるもあ
り、されど始より坐りて禮するを本式と
す、立ながら禮するは略なり、さて近よ
りて見合ふときは、其間を凡そ六寸空け
るが法なり、次の第三圖を見て知るべし
而して最早第三圖の場合に至らば互ひに
手の拇指を内へ屈め、透を見合ひて手を
出すに專らなるべし、但し此時は尤も防
ぐ心得あら
さるべ
ず、執るも
防ぐも卷首
に記せる執
る所の要處
喉、胸、
襟を、片
手にて執る
か、兩手に
て執るか、
何れにも褌を執る～し、又眉間を打ち、
脇を中てるものあり初めの執りかゝりに

（第三圖）

23

● Idori[7]: Seated Technique
Reishiki : How to Bow

Jujutsu instruction manuals are typically divided into chapters. If you look at a typical catalogue of techniques you will find the first chapter introduces Idori, Seated Techniques. Since these techniques are about fighting whilst seated, they are called Seated Techniques.

Illustration 1

First of all, as shown in the first illustration, both combatants will do a Rei, or bow of mutual respect. The way this is done is to begin standing about 1 Ken or 6 Shaku apart.[8] Both you and the Attacker seat yourselves in Agura, or cross-legged on the ground.[9] Your hands are on your knees as you look into each other's eyes.

---

[7] This is pronounced "E-dori."

[8] The author gives two measurements of distance, Ken and Shaku. One Ken 間 is 180 centimeters. A Shaku 尺 is 30 cm and 6 Shaku is also 180 cm. Another way to say this is there are 6 Shaku in 1 Ken.

[9] In the version of "cross-legged" shown, the bottom of the right foot is pressed against the left side of the left thigh and calf. Your left leg is tucked underneath. If you were wearing a Hakama while seated like this, the front leg would be concealed so it would appear as if the person was seated in Seiza. Keeping your front leg out in front makes standing up faster and easier.

How to Bow

Illustration 2

Since you are doing a bow of respect at this point and the technique has not yet begun, your thumbs should not be tucked inside your fingers. However, you should be on your guard.

Next, as shown in illustration 2, both combatants move toward each other. First, step forward with your right foot, keeping your hands on your knees. Then step forward with your left. In this fashion, both you and the Attacker approach each other.

Sometimes duels with start with both combatants standing in Soto-Hachimonji, or standing with your feet facing outward like the bottom of the Kanji for eight 八. You would then bow to each other before advancing and dropping down into Iai-goshi, or a squat, before seating yourselves Agura style, or cross-legged. However, the main way of doing things is to bow from Agura, while starting from a standing position is the abbreviated way of beginning a technique.

Both combatants, having closed the distance to each other, lock eyes. The prescribed distance is 6 Sun, 18 centimeters. [10] The explanation will continue in the next illustration.

---

[10] Sun (pronounced "soon") 寸 is 3 centimeters. 10 Sun make 1 Shaku and 6 Shaku make 1 Ken.

How to Bow

Illustration 3

As this third illustration shows, both combatants have their thumbs tucked against their palms, with the other four fingers wrapped around the thumbs. Both you and the Attacker are watching each other carefully for any opening. If either of you sees a gap in the other's defenses, your hands will move instantly. However, at this point it would be a mistake to devote your attention entirely to defense.

As was mentioned earlier in this volume, you should be considering carefully where you will grab. This could be the collar, either by the chest or neck. You must also be aware that your opponent will try to grab you. Any of these actions could be with one hand or both hands. You should be prepared to employ or react to any of the above.

In addition, the initial attack could be a strike to Miken, between the eyebrows, or a knee to Abara, the ribs. Your first move should not be a grab the shoulder, elbow, upper-arm or wrist. If your opponent grabs, you should seize the parts of the body mentioned above in order to free yourself from his grasp. Further, it is possible your opponent's first attack is a kick to the groin so you should be extremely cautious regarding this and remain on guard.

As for other advice, if an opportunity to strike the ribs arises, take it. If you think you can wrap up his knee, then wrap it up. These chances will come and go as you both attack and sweep away attacks.

⬤ Idori: Seated Technique
Migi Hiji Kaeshi: Reversing the Right Elbow
Illustration 1

柔術　坐　捕　十

肩、脇、二の腕、腕首などを執るべからず、これは執られたる時、敵の手を外す為めにすることもなり、又初めより睾丸を蹴りなごするこもあり、因て睾丸は殊に初は用心堅固にすべし、其他脇は其中に中てるなり、外しにも膝を繋けることも、執りかゝり、りたる時に起るなり。

◎坐捕

右脇挟し右の圖の如く睾丸に用心して互ひに六寸間に近より、遠を見合ひて、此圖の如く右なる受手は左なる使手の襟を右の手に執るなり、此時手を出すに心得あり、必ず前より手を廣げて執りかゝるべから

(第　一　圖)

Reversing the Right Elbow : Illustration 2

柔　術　坐　捕　十一

ぜ、敵の襟へ近づきて廣げ執るやうにし握拳に為もし居り、神速に執り掴むべきなり、さて此際、掛撃をかけざれば、充分力は出でず、故に開と撃かけて掴み執るべし、即ち開ご云ふ掛撃踏ともに、敵の襟に手のかゝり居るやう、如何にも神速にして眼の届かざる位にすべし、他の空手は膝に在れども睾丸を捲ふ心持あるを見るべし、さて使手は、斯く受手より我が襟を執りたる腕首を、此圖の如く右の手にて下より捕り、神速に左の手を次の第三圖のごとく上より受手の二の腕へ掛け、掛けや否や又次の第四圖の如く外し、其勢ひ

(第　二　圖)

Reversing the Right Elbow : Illustration 3

柔術坐捕　二十

に同時に左の膝を突き、右の足を投げ出して、受手の右の膝へ繋げ、繋けると同時に神速に、開と掛聲かけて第五圖の如くして左へ引き倒し、圖と曰ひて第六圖の膝は突き、此時使手の右の膝は突き、此るなり、此左の足は蹈げ出して蹈ばり、受手の右腕は使手の右膝の上に乘る。

此第一圖より第六圖までの變形を見れば、緩やかなるやうに見ゆれども實際は電光石火の如く神速の働きにて、見物人の眼も届かざる程なり、さて、受手が初めに使手の襟を捕るは、右の手と思ひて間違はされご使手より右の手を左の手にて受手の腕首を下より捕り二の腕を左の手

（第　三　圖）

Reversing the Right Elbow : Illustration 4

柔術坐捕　三十

にて上より掛くるを若し誤りて、左の手にて受手の腕首を上より執り、右の手にて受手の二の腕を下より受け掴めば、曰的の如くならず、此邊を間違へざるやう慣れ置くべし、又、初心の間は、足を繋くることを忘れ、思ふやうに引御せず、一成程足を膝へ繋け忘れたと後にて心付くことさあり、因て之は大事のこゝ思ひて忘れざるやうに熟すべし、此第三圖にて右の足を出す氣味あるを見るべし、此第四圖に於ては既に使手は右の足を受手の右の膝に繋けたり、學生諸君は物理を修得せらる故、物理を以て説かば曉り易

（第　四　圖）

Reversing the Right Elbow : Illustration 4 (continued)

　柔　術　坐　捕　　十四

じ、因て、槓桿の理を以て説くべし諸君
が識らるゝ如く、槓桿には力點、支點、
重點の三點あり、此三點の位置に由りて
物體の重心、體外へ出づれば其物體は傾
斜し、俯又出づれば顚覆す。柔術に於て
引き倒すも此理にて、力のみにて引き倒
すに非ず物體の重心、體外に出づるを知
るべし、されば此形に於て、使手の左右
の手にて靴り握れる所は力點、敵の身體
みれば、重心は体外に出でて、苦もなく引
は支點なり、即ち身体を支へて、力を用
倒し得らる、是れ柔術の柔にて、剛を倒
の因なり、又、受手の右の腕を、使手の
右膝へ上するは、何時にても折り得れば
なり其執り所、膝に上する所、一も徒な
るこそあらず、受手たる者の拙き者の劍
に遇ひたるよりも畏ろしきを知るべし、
左に因みに掛聲の理由を説くべし、これ
は聞き聲を掛くれば力出でて、圖と曰ひ

Reversing the Right Elbow : Illustration 5

　柔　術　坐　捕　　十五

て、伏せれば、甚だ極りよきには大に深
き所以あり、此掛聲は、開と聞こゆれど
も、實は聞にて、開圖の理より出でたる
なり、開は文字の意の如く開くゝにて
「ウンは圖づる事なり、口を圖づれば圖の聲
出で、口を開けば「ア」の聲
理より出で出でたり。
夫の伽藍に在る二
王門は、一個は口
を開き、一個は口
顯はしたるなり、
らず、開圖の相を
人は力を入れ
自然に「ア」の聲
出で、力を入
れて口を閉づ
れば「ウン」の聲出づ、又開は始まる聲にて
圖る終る聲なり、先きに圖と言ひて、後
に開とは止まらず、されば、開と言ひて

（第　五　圖）

Reversing the Right Elbow : Illustration 6

よりは、圖と言ふまで
開の餘聲は他に聞えさ
れども、其氣は續きあ
りて、圖と言ひて其聲
止むものなり、都て伏
せる時さ投るさきは、
此掛聲をかけることに
て、此他眉間、肋
を打つ時、

睪丸を蹴る時、
何時にても力
を入るゝさきは、
自然に此聲
出るものなり、
然る故に受止
むる時、拒ぐ時、圖の聲出づるも當然の
事なり、これは何にも有ることなり。

●坐捕
引返し
これは誠に手の少なき、素早き捕り方な
り、二變して勝頁の付く形なれば、其神
速なるこさ、實に電光石火も啻ならずさ
謂ふべし、これは受手より使手の襟を右

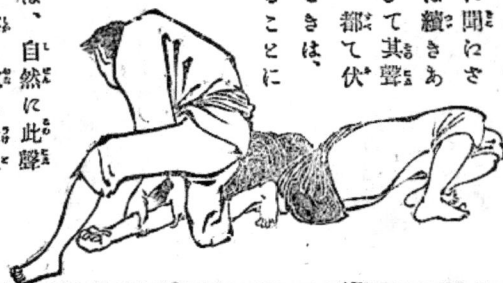

（第　六　圖）

● Idori: Seated Technique
Migi Hiji Kaeshi: Reversing the Right Elbow

Illustration 1

The illustration shows, both combatants advance until they are 6 Sun, 18 centimeters apart, all the while being careful to guard their groin. You and the Attacker each look for a Suki, or opening, in the other's defenses. In this illustration you are on the left and the Attacker is on the right. He reaches out and grabs your collar with his right hand.

There is an important lesson here about how to grab. Whenever you reach out to seize your opponent, do not do so with an open hand. Instead, only open your hand as it nears your opponent's collar. Until you are about to grab hold, your hand should be in a fist. Then, seize your opponent's collar with Shinsoku "Divine Swiftness."

When doing this sort of attack, failing to use a Kakegoe, a shout unifying your movement and intent, will mean you will not be able to apply as much power as necessary. Thus, you should use a Kakegoe of *Ya!* when applying this technique.

In other words, the Attacker should be shouting *Ya!* as he grabs your collar. This action should be done with Shinsoku speed, faster than the eye can register. It is important to note that his other hand, which is empty, is resting on his knee in order to protect his groin.

● Idori: Seated Technique
Migi Hiji Kaeshi: Reversing the Right Elbow

Illustration 2

The Attacker has grabbed your collar with his right hand. You respond by grabbing his elbow from below with your right hand. This is shown in the illustration. With divine swiftness grab his Ninoude, or bicep, from above with your left hand. This is shown in the third illustration. The moment you grab his bicep, force his arm off your chest as shown in the fourth illustration.

Using that momentum, you next press your left knee into the ground and thrust your right foot out, planting it up against the Attacker's right knee. As soon as you plant your right foot by his knee, shout a Kakegoe of *Ya!* and pull him down to your left. This is shown in the fifth illustration. Shove him into the ground with a Kakegoe of *Un!* This is shown in the sixth illustration. When doing this, press your right knee into the ground and have your left foot planted on the ground. You should have the Attacker's right arm on top of your right knee.

● Idori: Seated Technique
Migi Hiji Kaeshi: Reversing the Right Elbow

Illustration 3

When you are looking at how the figures move starting from the first illustration and ending with the sixth illustration, it may seem as if the action is happening slowly. However, in reality the actions should all be as fast as lightning. Your movements should not even register in the eye of an observer.

Returning to the technique, the Attacker has reached out and unhesitatingly grabbed your collar with his right hand. You responded by grabbing the Attacker's elbow from below with your right hand, and now, as shown in Illustration 3, you seize his bicep from above with your left hand.

It is important to remember that if you make a mistake and grab the Attacker's elbow from above with your left hand and his bicep from below with your right hand, you will not achieve your goal of pulling the Attacker down. You should train this technique so that this sort of error does not occur.

● Idori: Seated Technique
Migi Hiji Kaeshi: Reversing the Right Elbow

Illustration 4

Beginners will often forget to plant their foot beside the Attacker's knee, which will make it difficult to pull down an opponent. Later, beginning students will often say something along the lines of, "Now I understand, I forgot to plant my foot by his knee!" Clearly this is an important point that should be drilled into learners so that they do not forget.

In the previous third illustration, note how the picture shows you are readying to move your right leg forward. Then in the fourth illustration, shown above, you have already planted your right foot beside the Attacker's right knee. Surely students would very much like to hear the natural law that makes this possible. As it turns out describing how this works through natural law makes the understanding easier.

So I will explain this technique using the principle of the lever. As you all know, there are three parts to a lever: where you apply force, the fulcrum and the load. Using these three points it is possible to shift the center of gravity of a body outside itself, causing that body to tip. Then if more force is applied, it will flip over.

● Idori: Seated Technique
Migi Hiji Kaeshi: Reversing the Right Elbow

Illustration 5

Jujutsu uses this principle to pull opponents down. It does not rely solely on strength to achieve this, rather it uses fundamental principles to naturally topple them. Understand that Jujutsu shifts your opponent's center of gravity outside himself.

Thus, in this Kata, the points you grab with your left and right hands are where you are applying force. The Attacker's body is the load and the point where your right foot rests against his right knee is the fulcrum. Thus, with your body providing stability you apply power and the Attacker's center of balance shifts outside his body, by doing this you can easily topple him. This is how the soft and flexible can topple the strong and rigid in Jujutsu.

Further, by placing the Attacker's right arm on top of your knee, you can break it whenever you like. Once you have his arm on your knee, there is really nothing he can do. Most people would rather fight a man who was clumsy with a sword than be at someone's mercy like this.

● Idori: Seated Technique
Migi Hiji Kaeshi: Reversing the Right Elbow

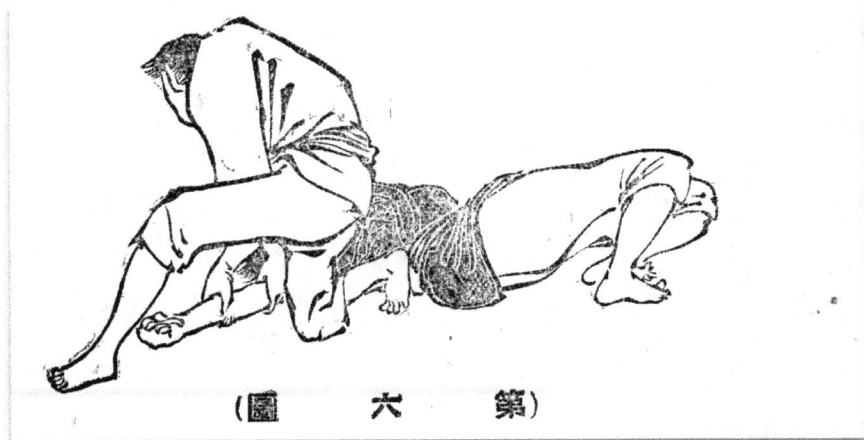

（第　六　圖）

Illustration 6

Next, a discussion of Kakegoe would be prudent. You should shout *Ya!* to put power in an attack and use *Un!* when pressing your opponent into the ground. This will make each move more precise. Veteran Jujutsu practitioners always use Kakegoe shouts.

When using this Kakegoe, it sounds like you are saying *Ya!* but you are actually saying *Ah!* The origin of these sounds is Ah-Un 開闔. The Kanji used for *Ah!* is Open 開 while the Kanji used for *Un!* is Closed 闔. When you open your mouth you say *Ah!* and when you close your mouth you say *Un!*

You often see two statues guarding the front gates of temples, one of which has its mouth open and another that has its mouth closed. This is doing none other than showing *Ah-Un.* When you put power into your body with your mouth open you will naturally say *Ah!* When you put power into your body with your mouth closed you say *Un!* In addition, *Ah!* is the sound of beginning and *Un!* is the sound of something ending. If you start off by saying *Un!* and then later say *Ah!* then there will be no ending.

Thus, you start a technique by saying *Ah!* and continue the sound, making it reverberate until it is time for you to say *Un!* Do this even if the people around cannot hear it. You say *Un!* to stop both the sound and the technique.

Thus, anytime you throw or pull an attacker down, these Kakegoe should be used. Also when striking to Miken, between the eyebrows, kneeing the ribs or kicking your opponent in the groin, anytime you are putting strength into your body, you should naturally voice these sounds. It follows that when you are blocking or shoving an opponent you should make the sound *Un!* This applies to all techniques.

● Idori: Seated Technique
Hiki Kaeshi: Pulling and Rolling Over
Illustration 1

柔術坐捕　十七

の手にて執るを、使手は右の手にて此圖
の如く・執りたる受手の右の腕首を、下
より取り上げ外し同時に右膝を立て左の
膝を突き
夫れより
使手
は、左の
第二圖
のごと
く、右
の足を
退きな
がら體を輾し、左の手の肱を、
受手の脇三枚へ、開と曰ひて中て、圖さ
日ひて突き倒すなり。斯くすれば使手の
働き、素早き故、之を防ぐ間あらず、如
何にともすべからざるなり、是等を「中
て」といふ、睪丸を蹴るも、眉間を打つも
凡そ急所を中てゝ悶絶せしめ或は即死せ

（第　一　圖）

Pulling and Rolling Over : Illustration 2

柔術立合　十八

しむるを「中て」ご
謂ふ、前
の肱が
しなご
げ」と
は「投
謂ふな
り。

◎立合　禮式
これにも禮式あり、
これは坐捕の如く坐
して體せず、立合は立ちて柔術を捕り合
ふこゝなれば立ながら禮するなり、これ
も双方の間六尺空け、足は外八文字に蹈
み、次の頁の圖の如く、兩手を腰へ當て
ゝ見合ひ、一禮して、間六寸まで近よる
なり。圖は「行違ひ」の始に揭ぐ。
◎立合
左行違ひ
次の圖は前に記したる禮式をせじ所の形

（第　二　圖）

● Idori: Seated Technique
Hiki Kaeshi: Pulling and Rolling Over

Illustration 1

There are not a lot of steps in Pulling and Rolling Over and the technique is done very quickly. Since this Kata only has two steps before you take down your opponent, they must be done with Shin-shoku, or divine swiftness. Your actions should be as fast as lightning, or how a spark emerges from a rock after it is struck with a sword.

The Attacker seizes your collar with his right hand. You respond by grabbing his wrist with your right hand from below. Shove his arm up and off as you put pressure on your left knee and stand up on your right foot. Next, as shown in the second illustration, you rotate your body clockwise as you pull your right foot back. Strike to Abara Sanmai, the third rib, with your left elbow. Shout *Ya!* as you do this and then *Un!* as you shove him to the ground.

● Idori: Seated Technique
Hiki Kaeshi: Pulling and Rolling Over

Illustration 2

These movements of yours should be so fast that the Attacker has no chance to defend. Ensure that not only this technique, but all your strikes are done in this fashion. This also applies to kicks to the groin and punches aimed between the eyebrows. Any strike to these Kyusho, or vital points, can result in the opponent being rendered unconscious or even suddenly dropping dead. These attacks are all referred to as Ate, or strikes.

As shown in this technique, you are forcing your opponent's elbow over and thus this action is called a Nage, or throw.[11]

---

[11] The author does not mention rotating the elbow over during the description. The Attacker is also shown raising his left arm to protect his armpit from your strike to his ribs.

● *Idori : Migi Tori Kaeshi*
Seated Technique : Responding to a Right Grab
Illustration 1

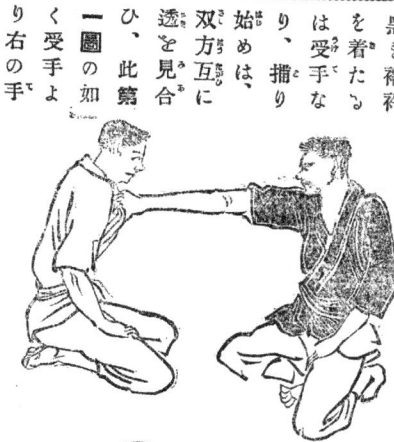

Seated Technique : Responding to a Right Grab
Illustrations 2 & 3

Seated Technique : Responding to a Right Grab
Illustration 4

捕　　坐　　術　　柔　　　　十五

ご、開の聲の如く高からず、圖と口の中
やうに思ふ、これは圖とは日ひ居るなれ
倂し、開とは出づれど、圖とは出でざる
きには此掛聲は自然に出づるものなり、
開闔、即ち開き圖づるの理にて、斯ると
開闔は文字の如く

開と
り、
法な
るが
伏せ

聲を掛け、
圖と日ひて
と日ひて掛け、
ときは、開
引き倒し、又は投ぐる

は定まり、使手の勝ちとなるなり、總て
には圖と日ひて伏せたらば是れにて勝負
ば、眞劍勝負ならば腕を折るなり、稽古
れば使手は其腕を折ること思ひの儘なれ

（第　四　圖）

Seated Technique : Responding to a Right Grab
Illustration 5

五十一　　捕　　坐　　術　　柔

心得べし、
眼を注けて
り方に能く
つき、其執
首を執る手
其初めの腕
右腕を執る
手が受手の
第二圖の使

盞あるなり
に於ては大
力を用ゐる
氣合抜けず
の如く續きて
一と氣に纏の

ひて、圖と止むるまでは、力の氣合が、
結局つかず、又、實益に於ても、開と日
のは圖と日ひて伏せるべし、然なくては
しながら、投げ又は引き倒して伏せるも
にて日ふが故、他へは聞ねざるなり、倂

42

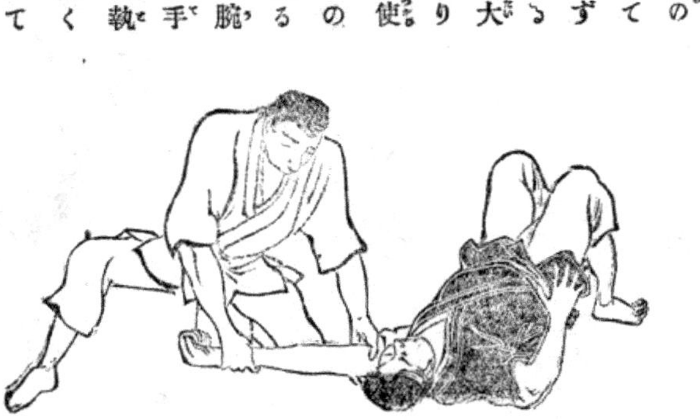

● *Idori : Migi Tori Kaeshi*
Seated Technique : Responding to a Right Grab

Illustration 1

Idori, seated techniques, are so named because they are all done while seated. You and the Attacker stand about 6 Shaku, 180 centimeters, apart. You both do a Rei, or bow of respect. Another way to refer to the distance "6 Shaku" is "1 Ken," thus you can also say you are standing "1 Ken apart." From that standing position you drop into Iai Goshi, a squat, and then sit down in Agura style, with your legs crossed. Place your hands on your knees, then bow.

Starting from your left knee, began edging forward until you are 6 Sun, 18 cm, apart. As stated at the beginning of this document you are shown wearing white training shirt and the Attacker is wearing a black training shirt. This technique begins with both combatants staring at each other looking for an opening. The Attacker reaches out right hand and grabs your collar. This is shown in the first illustration

Responding to a Right Grab

(圖　二　第)

Illustration 2

You respond as shown above in Illustration 2. Reach up from below with your right hand and seize the Attacker's wrist. Your left hand reaches up from below to grip his elbow. Press into the inside of his elbow with the tips of three fingers of your left hand, from the middle finger down to the little finger. This will cause the Attacker's arm to go numb, allowing you to bend it.

Responding to a Right Grab

Illustration 3

Lift his arm up as you stand up on your right foot.

Responding to a Right Grab

(圖　四　第)

Illustration 4

Then, as the fourth illustration shows continue raising his arm as you stand up, pulling both feet together.

Responding to a Right Grab

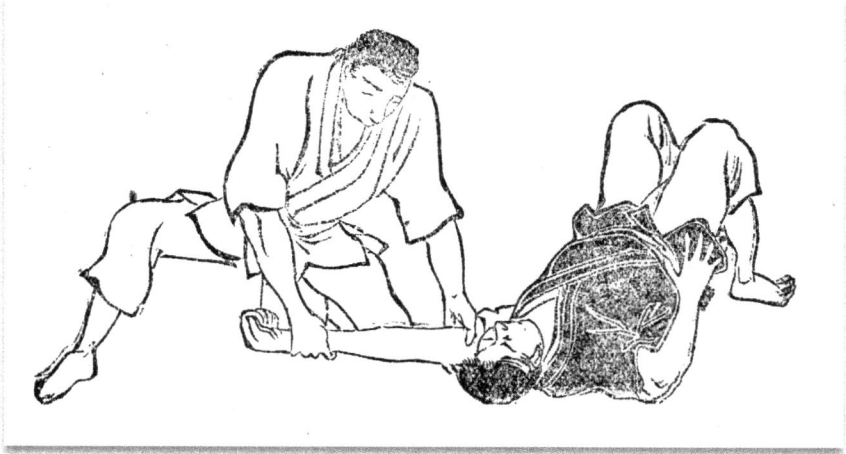

Illustration 5

Shout a Kakegoe of *Ya!* as you step back with your right foot. pull the opponent down as shown in Illustration 5 so that he lands flat on his face.

Since you brought his right arm down in front of your knee you could easily break it if you chose to do so. If this was a Shinken-Shobu, or fight to the death, you surely would have broken his arm.[12]

---

[12] Clearly the Attacker was pulled down onto his back in the fourth illustration. The illustration also shows you holding his left arm instead of his right. Below the illustration has been reversed, however this technique is still unclear.

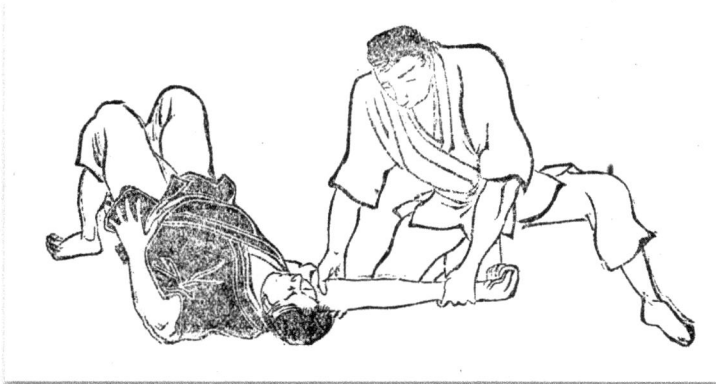

When training, you say *Un!* as you bring your opponent down, signifying your victory and his defeat. You should always shout *Yaa!* when throwing and *Un!* when pinning. This is the proper method. The Kanji are *Ah-Un* 開闔 but this combination can also be read *Kai-Ko*. This is describing "opening and then closing," or something "beginning and then ending" therefore these shouts should naturally be voiced when applying techniques. Some people feel that while *Ya!* is a sound you would naturally shout *Un!* is not.

My response is; since your mouth is closed when you are vocalizing *Un!* you are not making a loud noise like with *Ya!* Therefore those around you cannot hear it. So, whenever you finish a throw or pull a person down and pin them you should vocalize *Un!* This is the way Kakegoe should be used. By starting an action with *Ya!* and continuing that sound to until you finish the technique with *Un!* your power is maintained without lapse, like a continuous thread. This is the real benefit of Kakegoe.

Illustration 2

Illustration 2 shows how to grab the Attacker's right arm. You should pay particular attention to this important move. Note how you grip the Attacker's wrist and how your left hand takes his elbow.

If you do not set up your hands properly the technique will not go as you like and you will end up losing the encounter. Finally, note that the first move of this technique is seizing the Attacker's elbow from below. Do not forget to apply pressure to the inside of his elbow with the fingertips of the three fingers of your left hand. This pressure will cause his arm to go numb.

⬤ *Idori : Hidari Hiji Uchi Yoko Hiki*
Seated Technique : Striking the Left Elbow, Pulling to the Side
Illustration 1

Striking the Left Elbow, Pulling to the Side : Illustrations 2 &3

Striking the Left Elbow, Pulling to the Side : Illustration 4

四十五　柔　術　立　合

（第一圖）

（第四圖）

先を受手の左膝へ繋け
腕首を執りたる手を上よ
り持ちかへ、右の足を退
きつゝ、開と掛聲
かけて第四圖の如
く右へ引き倒し
鬪ご曰ひて伏せる
なり。此時受手の
左腕は使手の左膝
の前に在り、折る
事自在也
◎立合
　行ちがひ

● *Idori : Hidari Hiji Uchi Yoko Hiki*
Seated Technique : Striking the Left Elbow, Pulling to the Side

Illustration 1

The technique *Striking the Left Elbow, Pulling to the Side* begins with the Attacker striking with his left fist. He is aiming for Miken, the spot between your eyebrows. You respond by catching his upper arm with your left hand. This is shown in the first illustration.

Striking the Left Elbow, Pulling to the Side

Illustration 2

Next, as the second illustration shows, seize his right wrist with your right hand. While taking hold of his wrist stand up on your left foot.

(Standing up as you seize his wrist is a very natural motion.)[13]

---

[13] These brackets are by the author.

Striking the Left Elbow, Pulling to the Side

Illustration 3

Then, as the third illustration shows, plant the toes of your left[14] foot beside the attacker's left knee and shift your grip on his wrist so that you are holding it from above.

---

[14] The text says "left foot" but the illustration seems to show the right foot moving forward.

Striking the Left Elbow, Pulling to the Side

Illustration 4

Finally, step back with your right[15] foot and, with a Kakegoe of *Yaa!* pull him down to the right. This is shown in the illustration above. Pin him to the ground with a shout of *Un!* From this position the Attacker's left arm is by your left knee so you can break it if necessary.[16]

---

[15] This should probably be "left foot" since you are using your right foot to hold his left knee.

[16] Illustration 4 shows the Attacker's right arm being pinned. However, his initial attack was with his left hand. The image has been reversed below to show this. Also, it seems your left elbow should be on the Attacker's throat.

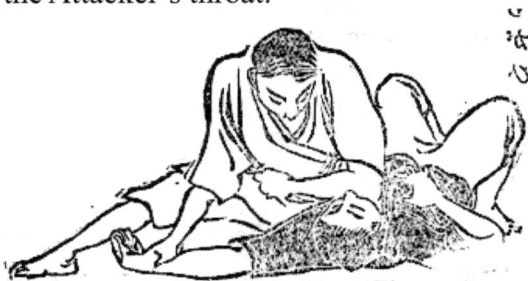

立合

Tachiai :
Standing Techniques

◉ Tachiai : Reishiki
How to Bow For a Standing Technique

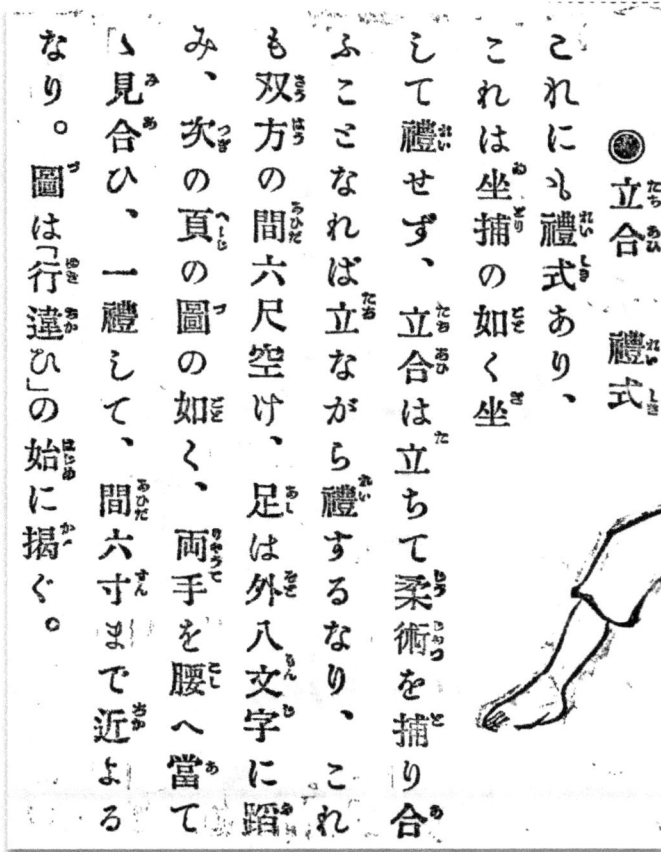

なり。圖は「行違ひ」の始に揭ぐ。
「ゝ見合ひ、一禮して、間六寸まで近よる
み、次の頁の圖の如く、両手を腰へ當て
も双方の間六尺空け、足は外八文字に蹈
ふこ°こなれば立ながら禮するなり、これ
して禮せず、立合は立ちて柔術を捕り合
これは坐捕の如く坐
これにも禮式あり、
◉ 立合 禮式

This is the etiquette for doing a standing bow. This is not like Idori, where you bow whilst seated. For Tachiai, Standing Techniques, you will be doing Jujutsu from a standing position so the Rei, or bow, will also be from a standing position. Both combatants should stand with their feet in Soto-Hachimonji about 6 Shaku, 180 centimeters apart. This is shown on the following page. Your hands should be on your hips as you stare into each other's eyes. After bowing, advance to within 6 Sun, 18 centimeters. The first illustration will show how to begin the first technique Yuki-chigai, Crossing Paths.

● Tachiai : Hidari Yuki Chigai
Standing Technique : Crossing Paths on the Left
Illustration 1

て却つて敵の脇を中てる形なり。斯る際ひさまに脇を防へ中てんさするを、受け行違ひと云ふは、形の名のごとく、行違づき、左の第二圖のごとく捕り合ふなりちなり、此體終りて、左の足より進み近

に、若し中てらるゝ者に油斷あり、或は手に覺に無くば、直ちに圖さ曰ふか、叮 さ曰ひて郤死すべし、輕きも悶絶の患ひ十九 ⎰立合⎰柔術

Crossing Paths on the Left : Illustration 2

當防衛にて止むを得ざるなり。さて此捕り方は、受手より左の手の脇にて、使手の左の脇を中てんとするを、使手は其脇を左の手にて、右の第二圖の如くに受受くるや否や訊速に、次の頁の第三圖の如く、右の足を受手の左の足の外へ踏み十⎰立合⎰柔術

を免れず、然るを此圖の使手の如く、手に覺ありて惡しも油斷透間なくば、禍を免れて反對に敵を打ち伏すべし、即ち正

Crossing Paths on the Left : Illustration 3

柔術立合　二十一

体をかはして右の手の肱に手のて受手の左の脇を中てるなり。

◎立合　羽返し中て

羽返し中ては使手より受手の襟を執りたる両手を切り掂ひ受手は使手の睪丸を突かんとするを、其手を取り上げて、脇を中てるなり、其況鳥の羽返しに似て、返して中てる故に羽返し中てさ云ふこれは左の第一圖のごとく受手より、両手にて使手の襟を執るを、使手は第二圖のごとく脚迷に両手を受手の両手の間へ下より入れ、第三圖のごとく両方へ、開と日ひ

(第 三 圖)

● Tachiai : Left Yuki Chigai
Standing Technique : Crossing Paths on the Left

Illustration 1

This illustration follows the Reishiki, or the etiquette regarding how to bow, described previously. Once the combatants bow to each other, they start walking towards each other, starting with the left foot first.

The second illustration shows how this technique begins. The name of this technique Yuki Chigai, Crossing Paths, which is basically a description of what happens. As you and the Attacker are walking past each other, the Attacker tries to strike you in the ribs on your left side with his right elbow. You block this strike and hit him in the ribs.

Crossing Paths on the Left

Illustration 2

If you were to be struck, it would be because you were not on guard, or your hands were not trained sufficiently to respond. You would immediately grunt *Un!* or *A!* and immediately die. Even if you are not struck hard, you probably won't be able to avoid being knocked unconscious.

As this illustration shows, you were not caught off guard and your hand reacted properly. Now, since you avoided disaster you will switch the situation around and strike the Attacker, toppling him. In other words, this is a justifiable defensive measure you have been forced to take.

After blocking you then, with divine speed, do as shown in the third illustration on the following page.

Crossing Paths on the Left

Illustration 3

Immediately step forward with your right foot, so your leg is behind the Attacker's left leg. As you step forward, twist your body counterclockwise and strike him in the left ribs with your right elbow.

● *Tachiai : Ha-gaeshi Ate*

Standing Technique : Bending the Wings Back and Striking
Illustration 1

（第 一 圖）

柔　術　立　合　　二十二

り第五圖にて變ずるうち、圖に能く眼を
受手の右の腋を中てるなり、此第一圖よ
を引きて右の手の肱を曲げ、開き曰ひて
足を受手の右の足を繋け、受手の右の腕
のごとく靭り上げ、體をかばして、右の
ごとく受手の腕首を靭り、それを第五圖
の手の線點に速に神又は

て切りはらひ、受手の腕を執らんとする
に、受手は手早く使手の睾丸を狙ふ、使
手はそれを知る故、睾丸を掩ひて體を左
へ轉すを、受手は右の手にて使手の睾丸
を第四圖の如く素早く突かんとす、使手

Bending the Wings Back and Striking : Illustration 2

（第 二 圖）

柔　術　立　合　　二十三

し、又、第四圖に至りて、睾丸を掩ふこ
きとは大に異へり、是等にも眼を留むべ
此時の身體つきと、次の第三圖の身體つ
は、何時にても此手つきなりと心得べし
すに、兩手を外

も、これ
りて切りて外

入れ
れて、切るにも、圖のごとく握拳の手を
して見るべし、又、使手の兩手を上げ入
使手の兩手つき、足の出し方、總て注意
此の如しと知るべし、此時受手の腰付、
下にして執る、兩手の襟執は何時にても
にて執るは、右の手を上にし、左の手を
着くべし、初め受手より使手の胸を兩手

64

Bending the Wings Back and Striking : Illustration 3

二十四　柔術　立合

この大事なること、注意の密にして機を見ることの敏きこと、思ふべし、殊に使手が左の手にて受手の腕首を執りたる、其執りやうを見るべし、斯く内方より、逆に摑み執らされば、第五圖のごとくに

引き上ぐるこことの能はず倘ず眼を認めて観るべきは、受手の右の足へ使手の右の足を繋けたるところなり、斯くせされば、右の手の肱にて、受手の右脇を中つるの位置を得ざるが故なり、此注意と順序は、堅く記憶りて、常に怖

（第　三　圖）

Bending the Wings Back and Striking : Illustrations 4 & 5

二十五　柔術　立合

（第　四　圖）

右の手にて襟を執りて引き倒しも爲すを得るなり、若し引き倒すさすれば、夫れの坐捕にて、足を敵の膝に

（第　五　圖）

習ひ置くべき事なり、又、斯く足を繋けたらば、若し肱へを繋ぎ斯く足繋り、又、若し肱へを中て損ふとも

65

● *Tachiai : Ha-gaeshi Ate*
Standing Technique : Bending the Wings Back and Striking

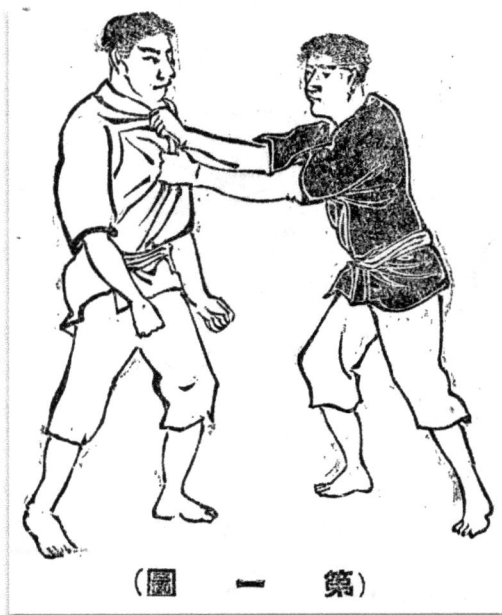

Illustration 1

Hagaeshi Ate, *Bending the Wings Back and Striking*, is a technique where the Attacker grabs your lapels with both hands. When you sweep his hands away, he then tries to strike you in Kinteki, the groin. You block and grab that hand and thrust it into the air before striking him in the ribs. The movements in this technique resemble a bird folding its wings. Since you fold the Attacker's arm back and then strike, this technique is called Hagaeshi Ate, *Bending the Wings Back and Striking.*

As the first illustration shows, the Attacker reaches out and seizes your collar on both sides. The second illustration shows how you rapidly thrust your hands up between his arms from below. As the third illustration shows, while shouting *Ya!* you sweep his arms aside. You attempt to seize his arms, but the Attacker suddenly punches, aiming for your groin. Since you were anticipating just such an attack, you drop one hand down to protect your groin as you rotate your body clockwise.

Bending the Wings Back and Striking

Illustration 2

The fourth illustration shows the Attacker's sudden strike to your groin. You respond instantly and seize his wrist, as shown by the dotted lines. Then, as the fifth illustration shows you thrust that hand up into the air, then step forward with your right foot, planting your right leg behind the Attacker's right leg. As you do this rotate your body counterclockwise and shout *Ya!* and strike him in the right ribs with your right elbow. Pulling on the Attacker's right arm with your left arm will make this easier.

You should look at how the movements progress from the first to the fifth illustration. Note that at the beginning, when the Attacker grabs your lapels with both hands, his right hand is higher, and his left hand is lower. Whenever you grab a person's collar with both hands, you should follow this hand placement.

Bending the Wings Back and Striking

(圖　三　第)

Illustration 3

As you look at the illustrations, observe everything, especially how Attacker's hips are positioned, how your hands are depicted as well as how your feet change position.

Further, your hands should be in fists when you slip them up in between the Attacker's arms and knock them aside. Not only should your hands be in this position when freeing yourself from the Attacker's grip, but this should be the standard way you hold your hands. Be sure to note that there is a big change in body position from Illustration 2 to Illustration 3.

Bending the Wings Back and Striking

Illustration 4

It is important to note how your right hand is shown protecting your groin in the fourth illustration. Understand that you need to be focused and prepared to respond deftly when the Attacker makes this strike.

When it happens, seize his wrist with your left hand. Be sure to look carefully at how the wrist is grabbed in this illustration. If you grab from the inside, you will not be able to pull his arm up as shown in the fifth illustration.

Bending the Wings Back and Striking

Illustration 5

Another thing you should look at carefully is how your right leg is placed against the Attacker's right leg. This placement is important since it allows you to line up your elbow strike to his right ribcage. The importance of this should be kept firmly in mind and reviewed whenever you train this technique.

The reason you place your right leg up against the Attacker's is in case your right elbow strike misses the Attacker's ribs. If you miss, then seize the Attacker's collar with your right hand and use that to slam him down. Then the technique becomes Idori, a seated technique. When you plant your leg by the Attacker's knee, his body becomes the resistance, your leg is the fulcrum and your hands are the application of power.[17]

As Illustration 4 shows, rotate your body clockwise and strike the attacker in the ribs on his right side. This technique began with illustration one and ended with illustration five. In this technique you avoided a kick to the groin as well as defended against an attack to the center of your eyebrows. You use the opponents own elbow to block his attack. Since your left arm was free you use that to strike your opponents take note of these deft movements.

(圖　一　第)　(圖　二　第)　(圖　三　第)

右の手にて襟を執りて

(圖　四　第)

(圖　五　第)

[17] The Attacker is shown blocking your strike. This is probably for training purposes.

● *Tachiai : Yuki Chigai*
Standing Technique : Crossing Paths
Illustration 1

（第　一　圖）

合　立　術　柔　　五十四

先を受手の左膝へ繋け、腕首を執りたる手を上より持ちかへ、右の足を退きつゝ、開と掛聲かけて第四圖の如く右へ引き倒し、圖に曰ひて伏せるなり。此時受手の左腕は使手の左膝の前に在り、折る事自在也。
◎立合　行ちがひ

（第　四　圖）

Standing Technique : Crossing Paths Illustration 2

五十五　　合　立　術　柔

これは受手より第一圖の如く右の手にて使手の左脇を中てんとするを、使手は右の手にて其肱を執りて防ぎ、神速に其肱を上げながらに体を右へ轉し第二圖の如く足を踏みかへ、左の肱にて受手の右脇を中てるなり。行ちがひの際には誠に早速の働きなり、これは中てらるゝを防ぐ心得さ、防ぎながらに、反對に敵を中てるの術なれば、簡單なる名法と謂ふべし。若し實際に斯ることあらむとき、正當防衛の爲めに斯る心得置くべきことなり。

（第　二　圖）

72

● *Tachiai : Yuki Chigai*
Standing Technique : Crossing Paths

Illustration 1

This technique is called Crossing Paths, it begins when the Attacker attempts to strike you in the ribs on your left side with his right elbow. This is shown in the first illustration. You respond by blocking his elbow with your right hand.

Standing Technique : Crossing Paths

Illustration 2

Next, rapidly shove his elbow up as you step forward with your left foot, rotating your body clockwise and striking him in the right ribs with your left elbow. This is shown in Illustration 2, above.

Crossing Paths must be done as fast as possible. The purpose of this technique is not only to block the Attacker's elbow strike but to flip the situation around and strike the Attacker. Understandably, this method is well-known among martial artists. This technique will be extremely useful as an appropriate method of self-defense against a sudden attack.

⬤ *Tachiai : Hidari Morote Kaeshi*
Standing Technique : Two Handed Takedown, Left Side
Illustrations 1 & 2

Two Handed Takedown, Left Side Illustration 3

● *Tachiai : Hidari Morote Kaeshi*
Standing Technique : Two Handed Takedown, Left Side

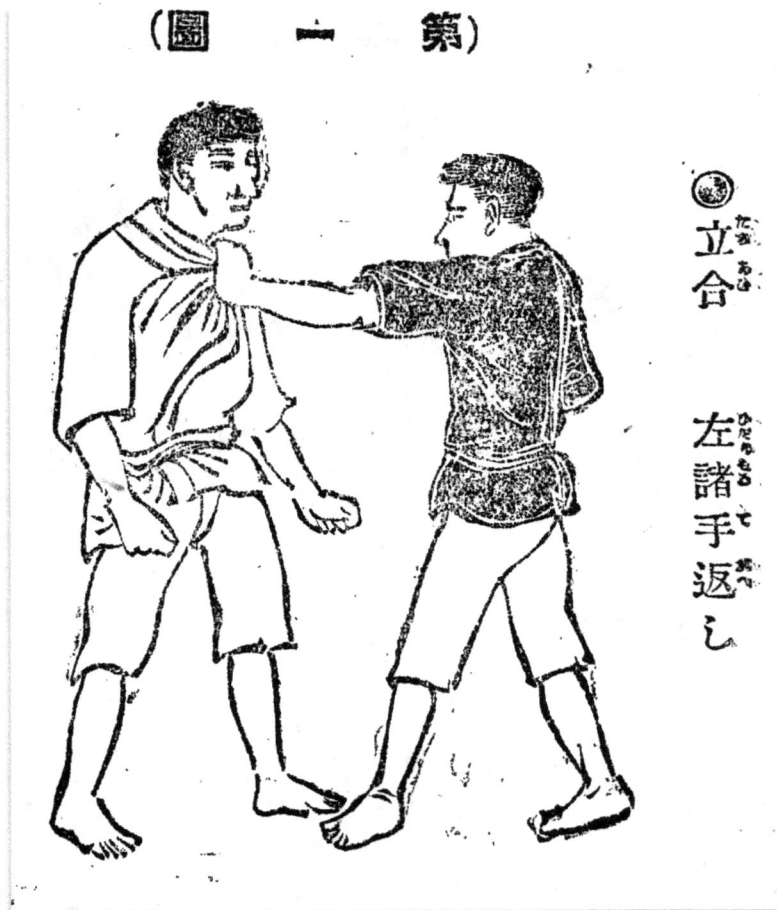

(圖 一 第)

◉立合

左諸手返し

Illustration 1

A standing bow should be done before beginning a standing technique. After the bow, both you and the Attacker stand opposite each other with your feet in Soto Hachi Moji, or with the toes pointed outward like the bottom of the Kanji eight 八. This technique, *Two Handed Takedown, Left Side* begins with the Attacker grabbing your collar with his left hand. This is shown in Illustration 1, above.

76

Two Handed Takedown, Left Side

Illustration 2

You respond as shown in the second illustration. Grab his wrist with your left hand and shove it up as you step forward with your right foot. You should end up with your right leg against the back of his left leg. Then immediately seize the back of his collar with your right hand.

Two Handed Takedown, Left Side

Illustration 3

As the third illustration shows shout *Ya!* as you pull him back and to the right. Shout *Un!* as you pin him to the ground.

As the illustration shows, you should be pushing into the Attacker's neck with your right elbow. From this position you have complete freedom to break his left arm, strike him between the eyebrows, strangle him or kill him in any way you choose.

中段

Chudan :
Mid-Level Techniques

● *Chudan: Unzan*
Mid-level Technique: Cloudy Mountain
Illustration 1

（第　一　圖）

柔　術　中　段　　二十六

繋けたるが如く、敵の身體は重點にて足
は支點、手は力點と知るべー。
●中段　雲山
中段も立合のごく、立ちて捕るなり、
故に其體式は、立合の體を爲すに異なら
ず、これは雙方近よりて、此第一圖のご
さく受手より
兩手にて
使手の兩
手を執る
を、使手
は次の頁の第二圖のごさく兩手にて、受
手の兩手を執り上ぐるなり、さて此第一
圖と、次の第二圖との變りを、能く眼を
留めて視るべし、受手の右の足へ、使手

Cloudy Mountain : Illustration 2

（第　二　圖）

二十七　　柔　術　中　段

の足のかゝりたるを視るべし、又、受手
の兩手を執りて上ぐることは、手先を上
げて摑めば、直に受手の腕首の摑めるこ
さ、第一の圖に於て見るべし、受手が一
旦執りたる手を離すは腕首を締めらるゝ
が故なり、さて夫れより使手は、此第二
圖のごとく右の足を受手の右の足へ繋け
体を轉じさま左の手を離し、直ちに其手
を次の第三圖のごさく後ろ
より廻
はして
受手
の頭へも
かけ、第
四圖の
ごとく引き倒すなり、其初め
右の足を第二圖のごとく受手の右の足へ
繋けたる後は、第三圖の點線の矢の方向
の如く引き倒すと知るべし、最早第四圖

Cloudy Mountain : Illustration 3 & 4

二十八　柔術　中　段

のことく引
き倒したら
ば、受手の
右の腕を折
ると
へ、
肩間
を打
つに
も使手の
隨意にし
て、受手

（圖）四
第）

使手が第三
圖にて、受
は到底免る
ゝこと能は
を、さて又
使手が第三
圖にて、受

（圖）三
第）

手の左の
手を離し
たるとき
受手は其
左の手を
働かすの
間合あら
さりしこ
とを知る
べし。

● *Chudan: Unzan*
Mid-level Technique: Cloudy Mountain

Illustration 1

The Mid-Level techniques are much like the Tachiai, Standing Techniques, since both you and the Attacker are standing, therefore the way you bow before beginning the technique does not differ from Tachiai. After the bow, you and the Attacker walk towards each other and the Attacker grabs both your wrists.

You respond as shown in the second illustration on the following page. Grabbing the Attacker's wrists from below you force them up. You should carefully observe the transitions shown between Illustrations 1 & 2, particularly how your right foot is placed against the Attacker's right foot. To seize the Attacker's wrists, raise your fingertips up and then grab.

Cloudy Mountain

Illustration 2

As the first illustration shows, the Attacker seizes your wrists, and you respond by grabbing his wrists. When you squeeze his wrists, the Attacker is forced to release. Next, as shown in the second illustration, you step forward with your right foot and plant it beside the Attacker's right foot.

Cloudy Mountain

Illustration 3

Let go with your left hand and rotate your body clockwise. As the third illustration shows, you wrap your left arm around the Attacker's back and grab his jaw with your left hand. Finally, the fourth illustration shows how you pull the Attacker to the ground.

You place your right foot against the Attacker's right foot as shown in the second illustration. Then, as shown in the third illustration, force the opponent down in the direction indicated by the arrow.

Cloudy Mountain

Illustration 4

The fourth illustration shows how you are positioned after you pull the Attacker down. From this position you can break his right arm, strike him in between the eyebrows or any other action you decide. The Attacker is completely under your control and has no recourse.

It is important to note that when you release the Attacker's right wrist with your left hand, to not allow the Attacker time to make use of the hand that has just been freed.

● *Chudan : Natsu Momiji*
Mid-Level Technique: Colorful Leaves in Summer
Illustrations 1 & 2

柔　術　中　段

合の禮に同じ
又坐して捕る
もあり、此形
の如し、初め
坐して捕るは
坐捕の禮に同
じく知るべし
專ら坐捕にあ
らず、又專ら
立合にあらず
因て中段と云ふ、
此第一
圖のごとく受手
より右の手にて
使手の眉間を打
たんとすると、
使手は左の
手にて受け
く受手より
第二圖の如
して近より遠を
見合ひ、此第一

（第　二　圖）　　　　　（第　一　圖）

Colorful Leaves in Summer : Illustrations 3 & 4

柔　術　中　段

（第　四　圖）

其腕首の脊にて眉間を打つを遮り止め、
手は左
の手に
て使手
の眉間
を突く
を、使
手は受
手の右
の肱を
執り、

右の足にて使
手の拳丸を蹴
るな、使手は
右へ體を轉じ
て拳丸を舉げ
て、右の膝の
如く右の膝を
立て、受

ひ、第三圖の
丸を掬

（第　三　圖）

Colorful Leaves in Summer : Illustration 5

柔　術　中　段

第五圖のごとく體を右へかはして受手の右の脈を中てるなり。第一圖より此處に至るまで、使手は睾丸を蹴らるゝを避け又眉間を打たるゝを防ぎ、其防たる腕首の脊を以て、受手が眉間を打つ手を遮り前に肱を防ぎたる左の手を空け其手にて敵を中てる其巧妙のはたらきを觀るべし。

◉中段　千鳥

此中段は立ちて捕るなり、體式には立合の體を用ゐるべし。さて其捕り初めは第一圖の如く受手より右の手にて使手の衿を執るを、使手は右の手にて次の頁の第二圖のごとく逆に其腕首を執り、第三圖

（第五圖）

● *Chudan : Natsu Momiji*
Mid-Level Technique: Colorful Leaves in Summer

Illustration 1

For the most part, Chudan, Mid-level techniques are done from a standing position. The way you bow is the same as for Tachi-ai, Standing Techniques. There are also Mid-Level techniques which are done from a seated position, like this one, *Colorful Leaves in Summer.*

It begins with you and the Attacker bowing to each other as described before. This way of bowing is neither limited to seated techniques nor limited to standing techniques. Thus, *Colorful Leaves in Summer* begins with you and your opponent bowing to each other before closing the distance between yourselves. You and your opponent are watching each other carefully to find an opening to attack.

As the first illustration shows, the Attacker punches to Miken, the center of your eyebrows, with his right fist. You respond by blocking this with your left arm.

Colorful Leaves in Summer

Illustration 2

As the second illustration shows, the Attacker next tries to kick you in Kogan, the groin, with his right foot. You respond by twisting your body clockwise and dropping your right hand down to protect your groin.

Colorful Leaves in Summer

Illustration 3

As the third illustration shows you stand up on your right foot. The Attacker punches to the center of your eyebrows with his left fist.

Colorful Leaves in Summer

Illustration 4

The Attacker is aiming to punch you in Miken, between the eyebrows. Defend against this attack by shoving the back of the Attacker's right elbow. This means his own right arm will block his left punch.

Colorful Leaves in Summer

Illustration 5

Finally, as Illustration 5 shows, rotate your body clockwise and strike the Attacker in the ribs on his right side with your left elbow.

This technique began with Illustration 1 and ended with Illustration 5. In this technique you avoided a kick to the groin as well as defended against an attack to the center of your eyebrows. You used the Attacker's own elbow to block his punch. Since your left arm was free, you used that to strike your Attacker's ribs. Take note of these deft movements.

Colorful Leaves in Summer		
1	2	3
（第　一　圖）	（第　二　圖）	（第　三　圖）
4	5	
（第　四　圖）	（第　五　圖）	

● *Chudan : Chidori*
Mid-Level Technique: Plover a Shore Bird
Illustrations 1 & 2

柔　術　中　段

（第　二　圖）　　の左てし轉を體くこごの

を受の又けへりろの受手を
受足左・掛頭よ後手を
・の、掛・り・・

（第　一　圖）

Plover : Illustrations 3

柔　術　離　れ　形

して斯く右の腕を
左の膝の上へ上す
れば折るは自在な
り、眞
劍なら
ば折る
なり。

●離れ形　締切
これは名の如く衿を執りて締めきるなり
締めきりて押し倒すなり、さて離れ形に
立ちて捕るなり、捕のはトめは、次の頁
の第一圖のごとく受手は右の手にて使手
の衿を執り、互ひに擧丸を摑ひながら、
グーイと締めて押し、一氣に押し倒さん

（第　四　圖）

Plover : Illustrations 4

柔　術　中　段

（第　三　圖）

手の右の足へ繋け、其れを支點さして開
ご掛撃をかけ、後ろへ引き倒し、闘と曰
ひて伏せるなり。此時には圖のごとく、
受手の左の手を使手の左膝に上せ、使手

は左の手にて受手の喉を押すなり。さて
第二圖の使手が下より受手の腕を執りた
る手つきを見るべし、斯の如く。執らざ
れば第三圖の如くならず、又左の足を受
手の右の足の後ろへ繋くる事を忘るべか
らず是れ無くば倒すを得ざるなり。而

● *Chudan : Chidori*
Mid-Level Technique: Plover[18]

Illustration 2　　　　　　*Illustration 1*

The technique Chidori, Plover, is done from a standing position. You should use the same bow as was shown in Tachi-ai, Standing Techniques. As the first illustration shows, this technique begins with the Attacker reaching out with his right hand to seize your collar. You respond by grabbing his wrist with your right hand.

This is shown in the second illustration.

---

[18] Chidori 千鳥 may refer to a Plover, a small oceanside dwelling bird notable for its rapid way of running along the beach searching for food.

Plover

Illustration 3

Next, rotate your body clockwise as the third illustration shows and wrap your left hand around his jaw from behind. Shift your left leg behind the Attacker's right leg.

Plover

Illustration 4

Using your left leg as a fulcrum, shout a Kakegoe of *Yaa!* as you pull him down on his back. Pin him with a Kakegoe of *Un!*

As the 4th illustration shows, you have braced the Attacker's right arm on your left knee while your left hand is pushing down on his throat. Note carefully how the second illustration depicts taking the wrist. Your hand should move up from below to take hold. If you do not grab his wrist in this fashion, you won't be able to take the position shown in illustration three. Also do not forget to plant your left leg behind the Attacker's right leg. If you forget this, you won't be able to pull him down. Note that by bracing his right arm on your left knee you can break it if you choose. If this were Shinken, a true fight, you would break his arm.

100

離れ型

Hanare Gata :
Separating Techniques

● *Hanare Gata : Shugetsu*
Separating Technique : Autumn Moon
Illustrations 1 & 2

柔術　離れ形　二十九

○離れ形、秋月

これもり立ち、禮は立に同じ、故になりて立、捕方は第一圖の如く受手より手を使く受手より右の手より手の襟を執るを、使手は右の手にて受手の腕首を執り、下より逆に右の手にて受手の腕首を執り、

（第一圖）　　（第二圖）

Autumn Moon : Illustrations 3 & 4

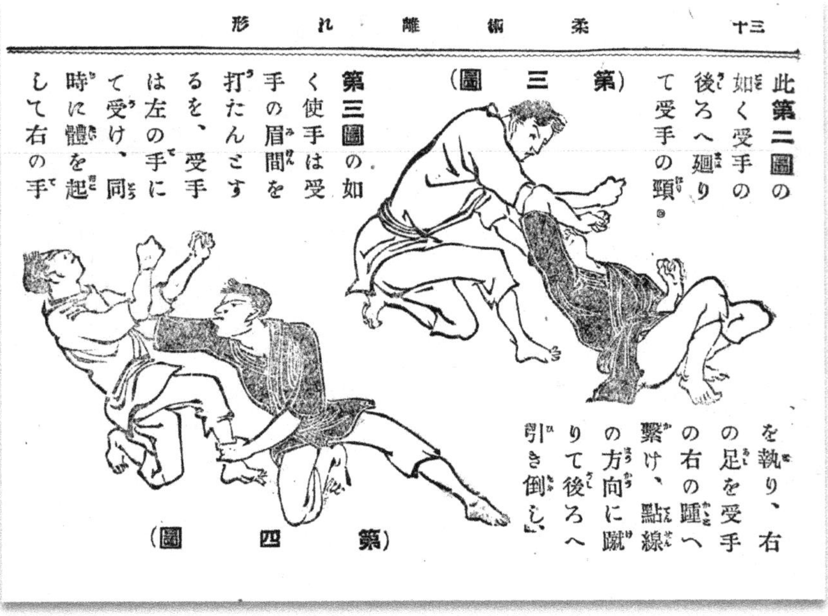

柔術　離れ形　三十

此第二圖の如く受手の足を受手の後へ廻りて受手の頸を執り、右の足を受手の右の踵へ繋け、點線の方向に蹴りて後へ引き倒し、

（第三圖）

第三圖の如く使手は受手の眉間を打たんとするを、受手は左の手にて受け、同時に體を起して右の手

（第四圖）

Autumn Moon: Illustrations 5 & 6

柔　術　離　れ　形　　　三十一

（第　五　圖）

にて使手の右足
首を第四圖の如
く執り、使手を
引くり返し、受
手は附きて起き
次の第五圖の如
くなりたるを、
使手は左の手に
て、第六圖の如
く受手の右の腕
を執り上げて起

き、右の手にて受
手の襟を執りて第
七圖の如く左へ倒し神速に
第八圖
の如く
右の手の拳に
て受手の眉間
を打ち、一旦
は危うかりし
使手も是に至りて遂に勝ちを得

（第　六　圖）

Autumn Moon : Illustrations 7 & 8

（第　八　圖）

（第　七　圖）

るなり、此形は餘ほ
ご入り組みたる形な
れば、心を沈めて第
一圖より第八圖まで
の變化を見る
べし、其初め
に使手より、
受手の腕首を
下よりかけて
執るは誠に心得事なり、是
れ後ろへ廻るに都合よから

んか爲め
なり、第
三圖にて

受手が、使手よ
り眉目を撃つを
素早く受け、出
でたる使手の右
の足を、くれり
と返りて執るさ
云ふは、如何に
も機轉なり、斯
くは能く素早
く働けども一は足
を執り、一は襟

● *Hanare Gata : Shugetsu*
Separating Technique : Autumn Moon

Illustration 2   *Illustration 1*

Since this is also a standing technique, the bow done at the beginning is the same as in Tachiai.

As the first illustration shows, the Attacker seizes your collar with his right hand. You respond by grabbing his wrist from below with your right hand.

As the second illustration shows, you circle clockwise around behind the Attacker and grab the back of his collar. Plant your right foot behind the heel of his right foot. Kick with your left foot as shown by the dotted line so the Attacker falls backwards.

Autumn Moon

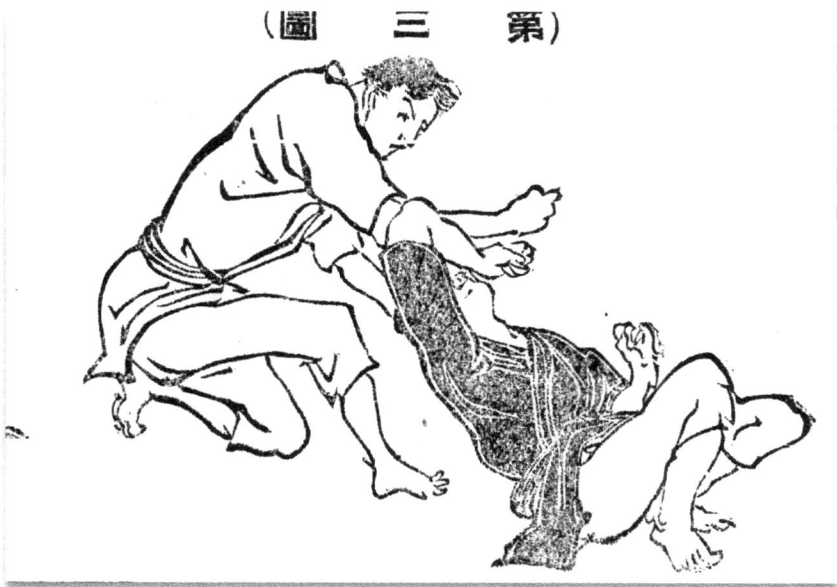

Illustration 3

As the third illustration shows, you attempt to strike the Attacker between the eyebrows, but he blocks this with his right arm.

Autumn Moon

Illustration 4

The Attacker immediately rises and seizes your right ankle with his left hand. He next seizes your collar with his right hand as shown above.

Autumn Moon

Illustration 5

Next, as the fifth illustration shows, the Attacker yanks your ankle with his left hand and shoves you with his right hand, forcing you down. You respond as shown in the following sixth illustration.

Autumn Moon

(第　六　圖)

Illustration 6

Grab the Attacker's right forearm with your left hand and force it up while raising your body.

Autumn Moon

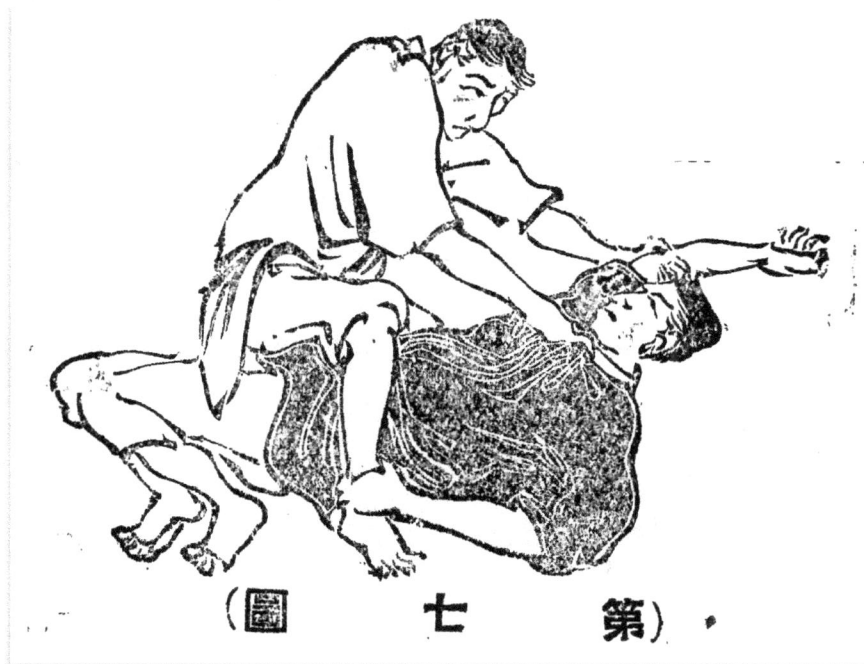

Illustration 7

Grab his collar with your right hand and rapidly topple him down to your left. This is shown in the illustration above.

Autumn Moon

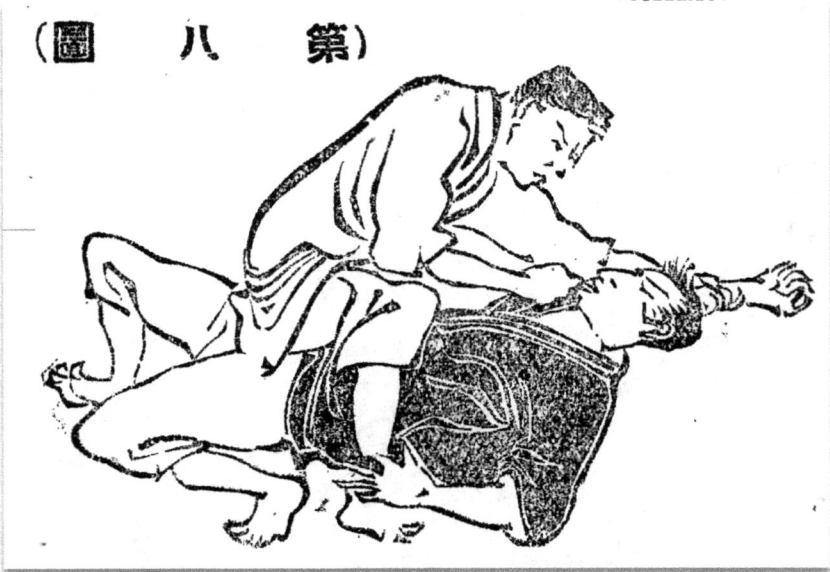

Illustration 8

As Illustration 8 shows, strike the Attacker between the eyebrows with your fist, enabling you to escape this dangerous situation. You have finally won this fight.

Though this technique is quite involved, remain calm and look carefully at Illustrations 1 ~ 8 and note how one movement transitions to the next.

Grabbing the Attacker's right wrist from below is a move that truly requires a lot of practice. This action sets you up to shift behind the Attacker, so it needs to be done deftly.

As the Illustration 3 shows, the Attacker quickly blocks your strike aimed between his eyes. By rolling over, he can grab ahold of your right ankle, which is extended out. The Attacker's counterattack is the result of quick thinking on his part. With one hand he grabs your ankle and with the other he grabs your collar. Since he is also guarding his groin, it is impossible for you to resist.

However, while the situation looks grim, in the end you grab hold of the Attacker's collar, pull him down and strike him between the eyes, resulting in his defeat.

◉ *Hanaregata : Shime-kiri*
Separating Technique: Escaping a Choke
Illustration 1

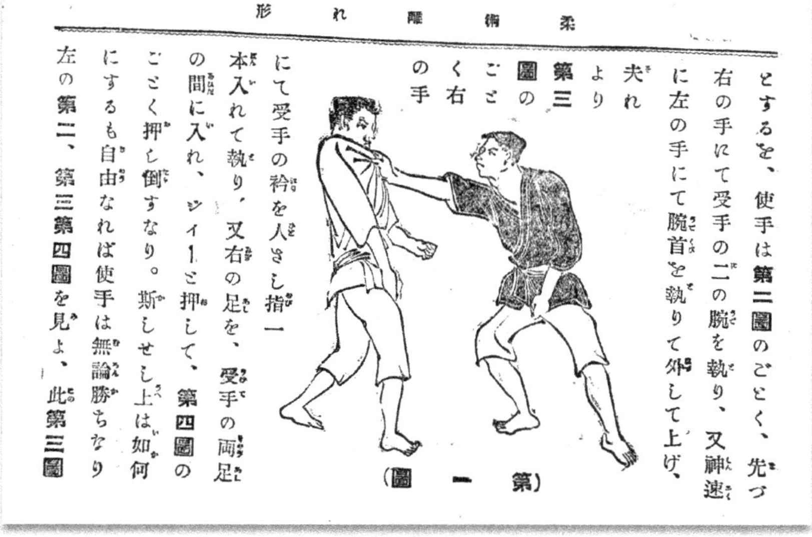
柔術離れ形

とするを、使手は第二圖のごとく、先づ右の手にて受手の二の腕を執り、又神速に左の手にて腕首を執りて外して上げ、夫れより第三圖のごとく右の手にて受手の衿を人さし指一本入れて執り、又右の足を、受手の両足の間に入れ、ジイーと押して、第四圖のごとく押し倒すなり。斯くせし上は如何にするも自由なれば使手は無論勝ちなり左の第二、第三第四圖を見よ、此第三圖

(第一圖)

Escaping a Choke : Illustrations 2 & 3

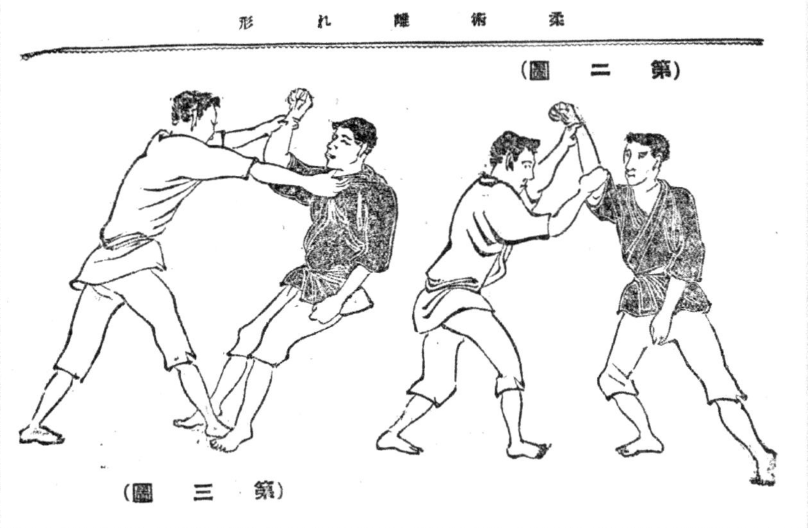

Escaping a Choke : Illustration 4

柔術離れ形

を能く見る
べし、押し
倒すさきは
足を繋けず
敵の両足の
間の正中に
入れ正しく正面に押すは
重心を体外に出ゑに外な
らず。

◎離れ形　引倒し

引倒しは大に異りたる形にて面白き形な
り、是まで足を蹴る形ば無かりしが、こ
れは使手より受手の足を蹴りて引き倒す
なり、離れ形は相撲にては離れ取のやう
なるものにて餘ほどかはりたる形あり、
此形などは其一なり、さて其捕り始めは
受手より左の第一圖のごとく右の手にて

（第四圖）

● *Hanaregata : Shime-kiri*
Separating Technique: Escaping a Choke

Illustration 1

The purpose of *Escaping a Choke* is clear from the name. The Attacker tries to choke you however you break free and take him down. Separating Techniques begin from a standing position.

This technique begins with Attacker seizing your collar with his right hand. Both you and the Attacker have one hand low, protecting the groin.

Escaping a Choke

(第　三　圖)

Illustration 3   *Illustration 2*

The Attacker then tries to shove you down with one push. You respond as shown in the second illustration by first grabbing his upper arm with your right hand. Then, with a quick motion, take his right wrist with your left hand and shove it upward.

Then, as the third illustration shows, seize his lapel with your right hand. Be sure to slide your index finger under his collar when you grab. Step forward with your right foot and plant it in between your Attacker's feet. Then, apply strong pressure until he falls. This is shown in the following illustration.

Escaping a Choke

Illustration 4

From this position above him you have total control so clearly you are the winner.

Look carefully at how this technique progresses, especially from illustrations three to four. Note how you topple your opponent in the third illustration. You are not tripping him, rather planting your foot directly between his feet before pushing straight into him. This action will cause his center of balance to go outside his body.

◉ *Hanaregata : Hiki-Taoshi*
Separating Technique: Pull-Down
Illustration 1

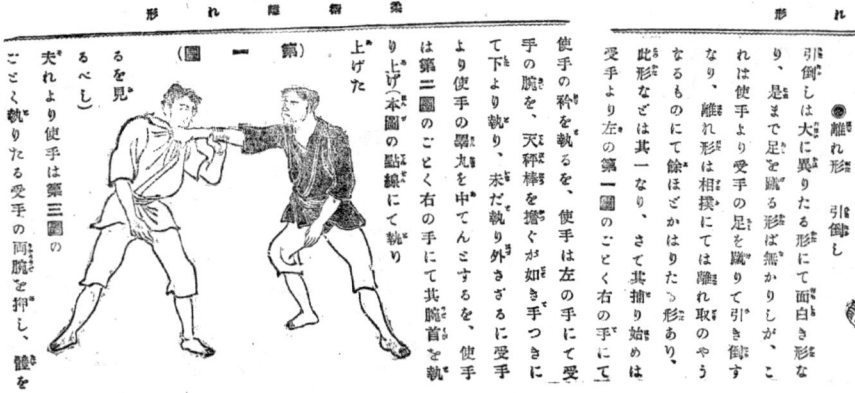

（第 一 圖）

柔 櫟 離 れ 形

れ 形

Pull-Down : Illustrations 2 & 3

柔 櫟 離 れ 形

（第 三 圖）　　　　　（第 二 圖）

Pull-Down : Illustration 4

柔　術　鑑　返　し

からず、殊に忘るまじきは　受手の左の
腕を執りたる其手を反對に持ちかへるこ
と肝要なり、此持かへは
動もすれば忘るゝものな
り、故に常に幾たびも捕
り習ひて、熟
練すべきこと
なり、斯くし
て伏せたらば
腕を折るさゝ
眉間を打つこ
も自在なり。

◎鑑返し
　これは柄捌の一科なり、されど柄を捕ら
ざる故、別に一科として記す、受手は使
手の帶したる刀の鑑を執りて締め上げ、
刀を用ゐる効を妨げ、押し倒して仕留め
んとするなり、然るに使手に油斷なく、
受手は反つて刺さるゝに至るなり。此初
めは次の頁に掲げたる第一圖のごとく、
使手が先に歩み行くぞ、受手は後方より

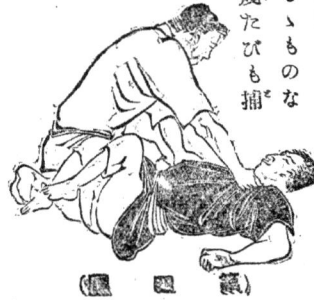

（鑑　返　し）

● *Hanaregata : Hiki-Taoshi*
Separating Technique: Pull-Down

Illustration 1

The technique *Pulling Down* differs greatly from the previous technique, however it is quite interesting. Until now there haven't been any techniques that use kicks. In this technique you will kick your opponent's leg and pull him down. This technique is like *Separating Away*, a technique used in Sumo wrestling.

Pulling down begins as shown in the illustration above. The Attacker seizes your collar with his right hand. You respond by grabbing his wrist from below with your left hand. Grab like you are holding a pole on your shoulder.

Pull-Down

Illustration 3   *Illustration 2*

However, before you can shove his hand off, the Attacker tries to punch you in the groin. You respond as shown in Illustration 2 by grabbing his left wrist with your right hand and shoving it up. (The dotted lines show the direction you should push his arm)

Next, do as shown in Illustration 3. You force his right arm up so both the Attacker's hands are above you. Then rotate your body counterclockwise as you step forward with your right foot. Hook your right heel behind the Attacker's right foot.

Pull-Down

Illustration 4

Pull his right hand down as you kick with your right heel. Shout a Kakegoe of *Yaa!* as you pull him down. Pin your Attacker with a Kakegoe of *Un!*[19]

While it is important not to forget to do this right heel kick, you must first remember to set the technique up properly by hooking your heel. Also, a fundamental part of this technique is reversing the way your left hand grips his right wrist.

Details like this can be easy to forget so you should practice this technique extensively. Having toppled your opponent, you are free to break his arm or punch him between the eyebrows.

---

[19] The text for this technique says to "hook your left foot behind the Attacker's left foot" however the illustration shows the right foot.

HISAMATSU SADAMOTO・久松定基

柄捌

Tsuka Sabaki :
Seizing the Sword Handle

◉ *Tsuka Sabaki*
Seizing the Sword Handle
Illustration 1

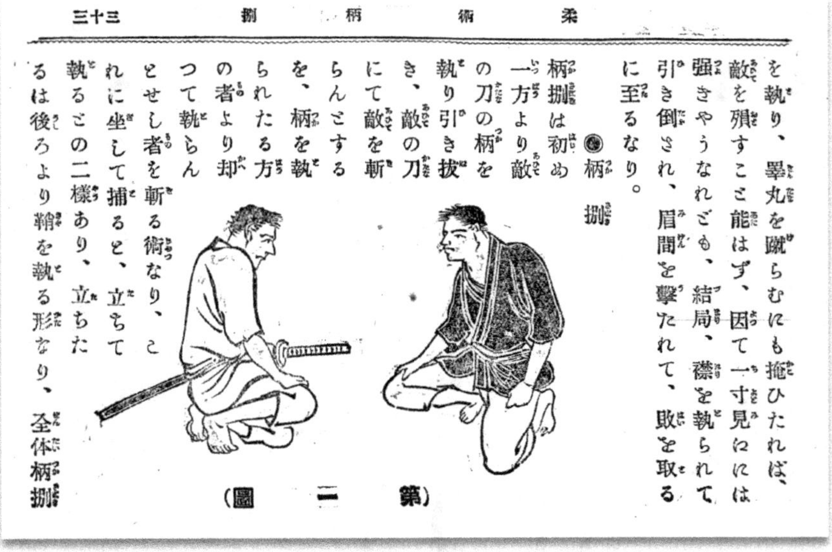

三十三　　　捌　柄　術　柔

を執り、睾丸を蹴らむにも掩ひたれば、
敵を殪すこと能はず、因て一寸見ぬには
強きやうなれども、結局、襟を執られて
引き倒され、眉間を撃たれて、敗を取る
に至るなり。

◉柄捌

柄捌は初め
一方より敵
の刀の柄を
執り引き抜
き、敵の刀
にて敵を斬
らんことする
を、柄を執
られたる方
の者より却
つて執らん
とせし者を斬る術なり、こ
れに坐して捕ると、立ちて
執るこの二様あり、立ちた
るは後ろより鞘を執る形なり、
全体柄捌

（第　二　圖）

Seizing the Sword Handle : Illustrations 2 & 3

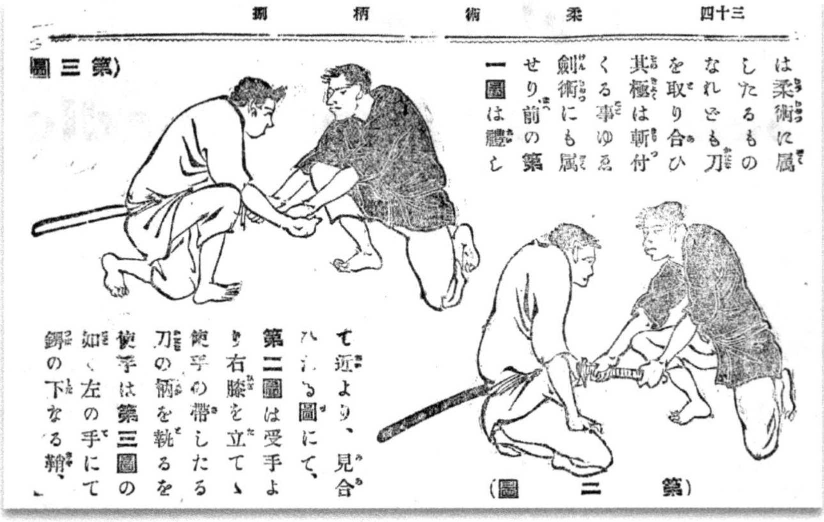

捌　柄　術　柔　　　三十四

は柔術に属
したるもの
なれども刀
を取り合ひ
其極は斬付
くる事ゆる
劍術にも属
せり前の第
一圖は體と

（第三圖）

て近より、見合
ひたる圖にて、
第二圖は受手よ
り右膝を立て、
徳手の帯したる
刀の柄を執るを
使手は第三圖の
如く、左の手にて
鍔の下なる鞘

（第　二　圖）

Seizing the Sword Handle : Illustration 4

柔　術　捕　捉　　三十五

即ち鯉口の所を持ち、右の手にて柄頭を
匕ひ持ち、第四圖の如くくれりと内へ捻
ぢ上げて強く放し、第五圖の如く神速に
柄をば受手の喉へ當て、又、第六圖のご
とく、神速に退きて抜き、受手の右の肩
を斬るなり、これも其速き
こと、電光石
火の動きなり
此術に達せん
さするものは
能く此第
一圖より
第六圖に
至るまで
の變化
其他容体何かご注目
すべし、第一圖は徒
だ體式のみなれど、
第二圖の受手が両手にて柄を執るに、若
し目的の如く敵の刀を抜き取りたらば、

（第　四　圖）

Seizing the Sword Handle : Illustration 5

柔　術　柄　捕　捉　　三十六

斬付くるに便なるやう、右の手を向ふに
し、左の手を前にしたるを見るべし、又
使手も右の手にて柄を握り、左の手にて
鯉口の所を持ち、敵の兩手を挾むは、我
が刀を捻ぢるに大丈夫なればなり、而し
て外へ捻ぢ上ぐるに逆なれども、内へ捻
ぢ上ぐるは力の運びよし、右の膝を上げ
て、左の膝
を突くは、
力を入るゝ
に都合よし、
受手は第四
圖の如く
にして使
手より七
ひ捻ぎ上
げらる、
を以て、
兩手は捻れて離れざるを得ず、捻れるに
由りて自づと離れ、離るゝ否や、捌は嚥
へご勢ひ向ふべし、此時受手より、強く

（第　五　圖）

Seizing the Sword Handle : Illustration 6

九十三　捌柄搦柔

抵抗する氣色あらば、柄頭にて喉を突き殱すを得べし、（捻ち上ぐるとき、刀の鞘の反り返りたるに眼を留むべし）さて又、受手が喉へ柄頭を向けられたるとき、抵抗せざるほどの者ならば此時氣後れして畏るべし、其畏るゝ透間を見て、其間一、髪、神速に體を退き、素早く刀を拔きて第六圖のごとく拔打に斬り附くるなり。併し此拔打は、別に居合拔の稽古を爲し置かされば思ふ樣に刀は拔けず因て居合拔の法を概説すべし、此稽古は先づ立ちて拔く事より習ふべし、

（第　六　圖）

● *Tsuka Sabaki*
Seizing the Sword Handle[20]

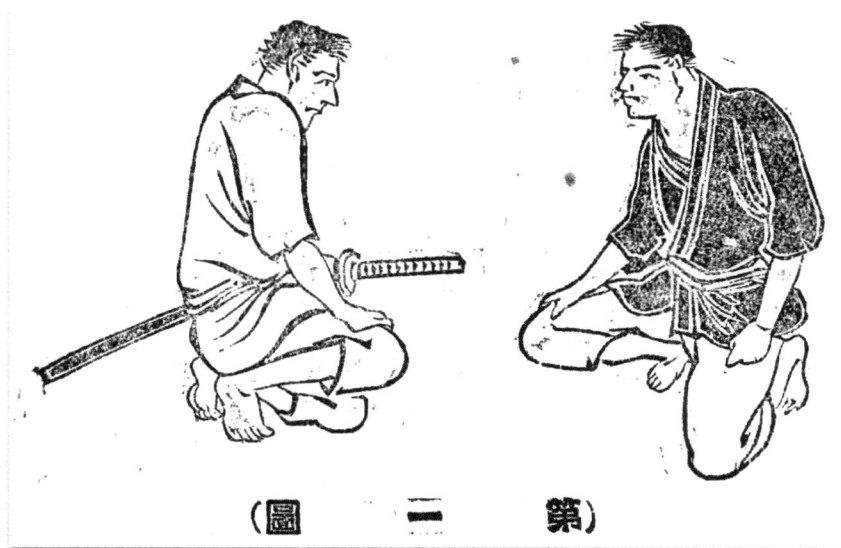

Illustration 1

There are two sides to the technique known as Tsuka Sabaki. If you are the Attacker then you are trying to grab the handle of your opponent's Katana, draw it out and then use it to cut down your opponent. On the other hand, if you are the defender then you are trying to free the handle of your sword from the person that has grabbed it and then draw and cut him down.

There are two types of Tsuka Sabaki techniques; seated and standing. The one being introduced here is a seated technique however there are also standing Tsuka Sabaki techniques. In standing techniques, the Attacker approaches from behind and grabs the Saya, scabbard, of your sword from behind.

---

[20] The pages of the next two techniques were completely out of order and required extensive reorganization. I've done my best to untangle what's happening in these techniques however I believe there may be at least one page missing.

Seizing the Sword Handle

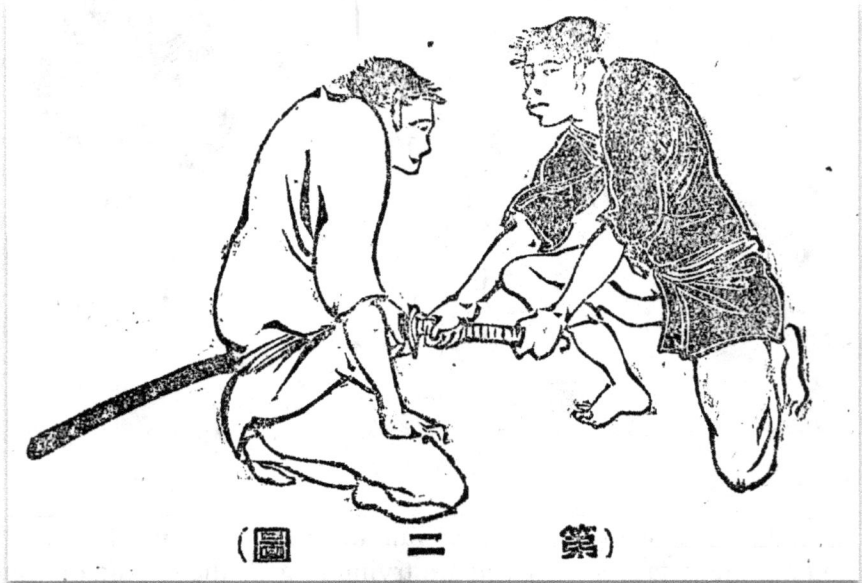

Illustration 2

Generally speaking, Tsuka Sabaki techniques are considered to be part of Jujutsu, however since the techniques are about struggling over a sword before the Attacker is cut down, they are also classified as Kenjutsu, sword fighting, techniques.

In the first illustration, both you and the Attacker have bowed and moved closer, while watching each other.

The second illustration shows the Attacker moving forward with his right foot and seizing the Tsuka, or handle, of your Katana with both hands.

Seizing the Sword Handle

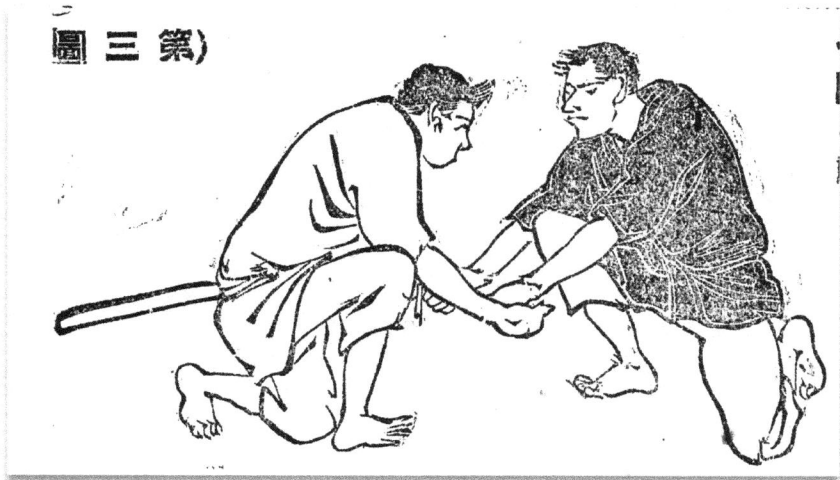

Illustration 3

You respond as shown in the third illustration by grabbing the scabbard of your Katana just below the Tsuba, or handguard. This spot, where the scabbard meets the handguard is known as the Koiguchi, carp's mouth. With your right hand grab the Tsuka-gashira, pommel.

Seizing the Sword Handle

Illustration 4

Next, as the fourth illustration shows, twist the handle firmly up and to the inside, forcing the Attacker's hands off.

Seizing the Sword Handle

(圖　五　第)

Illustration 5

Then rapidly strike the Attacker in the throat with the pommel of your Katana. This is shown in the fifth illustration.

Seizing the Sword Handle

Illustration 6

After that, the sixth illustration shows how you quickly drop back, draw your sword and cut down into the Attacker's right shoulder.[21]

This technique must be done as fast as a flash of lightning or as fast as a spark flying off when using flint and steel to start a fire. To become adept at Tsuka Sabaki, you should carefully observe the progression shown in illustrations 1 ~ 6, paying particular attention to the body positioning of each combatant.

---

[21] This illustration seems to show you cutting down on top of his head.

Seizing the Sword Handle

| Illustration 1 | Illustration 2 | Illustration 3 |

So, to review:[22] The first illustration is just the Rei, or bow. The second illustration shows the Attacker seizing the handle of your Katana with both hands. If he succeeds in his objective, he will draw the sword out and cut you down. Note that the Attacker has grabbed with his right hand forward and his left hand back.

| Illustration 4 | Illustration 5 | Illustration 6 |

You respond by scooping up the pommel with your right hand and the Koi-guchi with your left. With your hands on either side of the Attacker's hands, you will be able to twist powerfully. Twisting the handle of your sword clockwise is the wrong way. You will be able to apply more power by turning counterclockwise, or to the inside. As you twist, put your weight on your left knee and stand up on your right foot, which will add to your power.

From the position shown in Illustration 4 you twist and scoop up the handle of your Katana. The Attacker is forced to release his grip on your sword.

The twisting action forces the opponent back and, in that moment, you thrust the end of your sword out and strike the Attacker in the throat forcefully with the pommel, then drop back, draw your sword and cut down into the Attacker's right shoulder.

---

[22] This is the author retelling the technique.

● *Tsuka Sabaki : Uchi Iri*
Seizing the Sword Handle : Stabbing In
Illustration 6
(Illustrations 1~5 are the same as the previous technique)

（第 六 圖）

柔　術　柄　捌　三十七

より体をかはして持ちかへ、次の第六圖
のごとくに受手の胸を突くなり。此第五
圖の所にては
使手は右の膝
を立て、左の
膝を突けども
第六圖にて
は体をかはし
たるが故に、
左の膝を立て
ゝ右の
膝を突
けり、
是等の、捻ざ離すや否
や、後邊へ飛び退りて
神速に刀を抜くは、前
に記せる居合抜に熟せざるべからず、體

Illustration 7

（第 七 圖）

柔　術　柄　捌　三十八

のこなし萬端
居合の手あり
と知るべし、
總て勢ひによ
りて斯くなれ
ごも、齟齬す
れば反つ
て敗を取
る、慎む
べし〳〵。

●枕刀
これは寝入りたる所へ、忍び入りて、睨
ひ寄りたる曲者、夜具の上より跨がりて
寝たる者を害せむとするを、癖たる者は
刀を夜具の中に置きたるを以て、其曲者
を跳ね返して、拔打に其曲者を斬り伏せ
る術なり、これは柔術と撃劍と混じたる
ものにて、兩技活用の所爲と知るべし、
從前我も國武家の心得にも、深彼に臥な

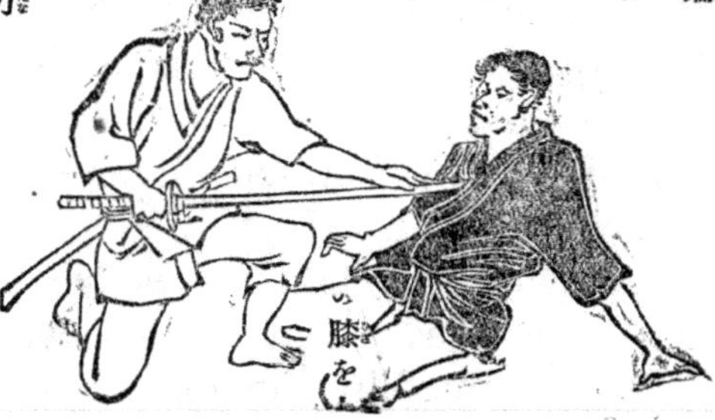

136

● *Tsuka Sabaki*
Seizing the Sword Handle : Stabbing In

Illustration 1   *Illustration 2*   *Illustration 3*

Illustration 4   *Illustration 5*

This technique begins the same way as the previous *Seizing the Sword Handle* technique. Steps 1 ~ 5 are the same as the previous technique.

The fifth illustration shows what happens after you twist the sword handle out of the Attacker's grip. The Attacker is persistent, so you hit him in the throat with the pommel of your Katana. (Note that when twisting the Katana, the curve of the scabbard is rotated down.)

In addition, when you strike a person with the end of the handle of your sword, it will cause even the most aggressive of opponents to hesitate. This will give you the chance, albeit one only big enough to fit a single hair in, to rapidly drop back and quickly draw your Katana. This is shown in the next illustration.

Seizing the Sword Handle : Stabbing In

Illustration 6

Quickly twist your upper body counterclockwise and draw your sword as shown in Illustration 6 before stabbing the Attacker in the chest as shown in Illustration 7.

Note that in Illustration 6 your left knee is down and your right foot is planted on the ground. As you move forward to stab, your body reverses and your right knee is down and your left foot is on the ground. This is shown in the seventh illustration.

The sequence of movements where you twist the handle, leap back and rapidly draw your sword requires intensive practice in Iai, sword drawing.

The reason is because all the body and sword movements are taken from Iai techniques. Since success in this technique requires speed, and any missteps will result in your defeat, you should practice carefully.

Seizing the Sword Handle : Stabbing In

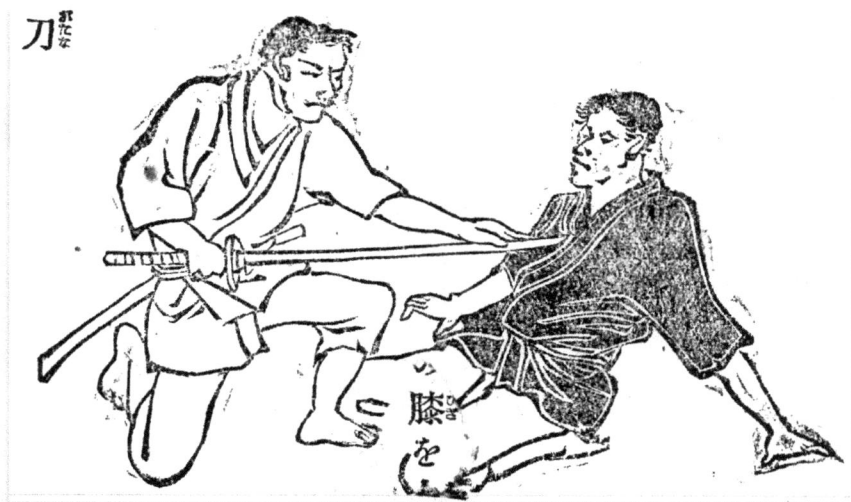

Illustration 7

The sixth illustration showed how you dropped back and drew your sword. Now, Illustration 7 shows how you stab the Attacker in the chest.

However, if you have not trained Iai, sword drawing, sufficiently you will find that you are unable to draw your sword in a timely manner, therefore I would like to introduce an outline of Iai training.

Description of Iai, Sword Drawing

十四　柔　術　祝　刀

足を外八文字に踏み、左の手にて鯉口を持ちながら三足出で、居合腰になり右の手を右の膝に置き、左の手を左の膝に置き、夫より刀を持ちヽへ、腰に帯し、左の手にて鯉口を持ち右の手を掌を仰向けて受くるやうにし、左の肩の所へ上げ、其手を下ろして柄へ掛け、其柄を握りて持ち上げ、開と日ひて左の足を退き、退きさまに抜き、柄へ左の手を添へ兩手にて持ち、一足進みて斬り、後へ飛び蹲りて大上段に構へ、柄を持ち下ろして持ちかへ、而して鞘へ收むるなりヽこれには收め方の法もあり、何分にも繁抜きて熟練すべき事なり。

◉柄捌　打入

これは初めは柄捌より始まるなり、故に第一圖より第四圖に至るまでは、前の柄捌第一形の圖に同じ、此圖は捻む上げて離してより直に後邊へ飛びて抜き、夫れ

● Iai : Sword Drawing

When doing Iai training, start from a standing position. Your feet should be in Soto Hachimonji, shaped like the bottom of the Kanji for eight 八. Place your left hand on the Koi-guchi and take three steps forward, before squatting down. This squat is called Iaigoshi. Place your right hand on your right knee and your left hand on your left knee. Then switch the Katana to your right hand and slide it into the left side of your belt. Hold the scabbard with your left hand by the Koi-guchi and turn your right hand so your palm is facing upward, as if you are going to receive something. Raise your right hand up to the height of your left shoulder, before lowering it onto the handle of your Katana. Next, grip the handle of your sword as you raise the handle up.

Shout *Ya!* as you draw your Katana, stepping back with your left foot as you do. Join your left hand to the handle of your sword, so you are holding it with both hands. Take a step forward and cut. Leap back and go into Daijodan, upper stance. Lower the handle, switch the sword around and sheathe the sword in your scabbard. There is a particular way to sheathe a sword, however you should practice drawing until you become proficient.

● *Kojiri Kaeshi*
Twisting the End of Your Sword : Illustration 1

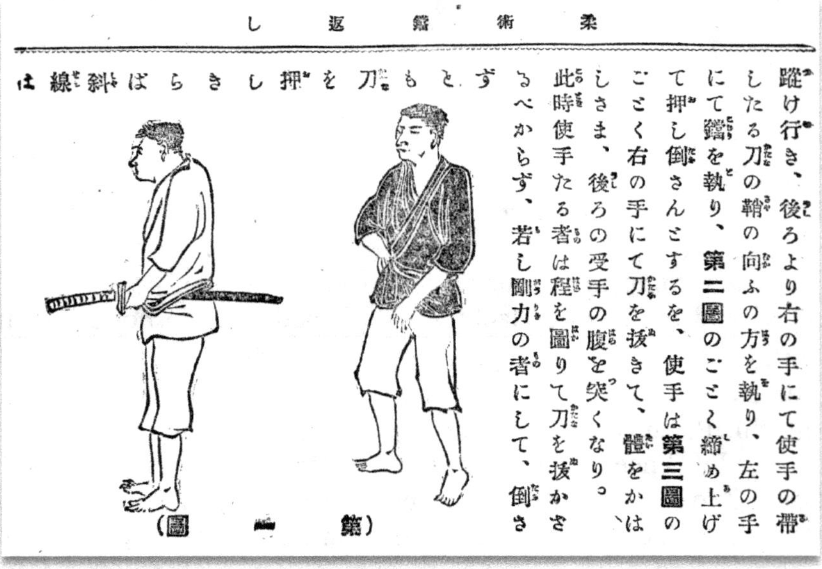

柔 術 鐺 返 し

は 線 斜 ば ら き し 押 を 刀 も と ず

蹴け行き、後ろより右の手にて使手の帯
したる刀の鞘の向ふの方を執り、左の手
にて鐺を執り、第二圖のごとく締め上げ
て押しさんとするを、使手は第三圖の
ごとく右の手にて刀を拔きて、體をかは
しさま、後ろの受手の腹を突くなり。
此時使手たる者は程を圖りて刀を拔かさ
るべからず、若し剛力の者にして、倒さ

Twisting the End of Your Sword : Illustrations 2 & 3

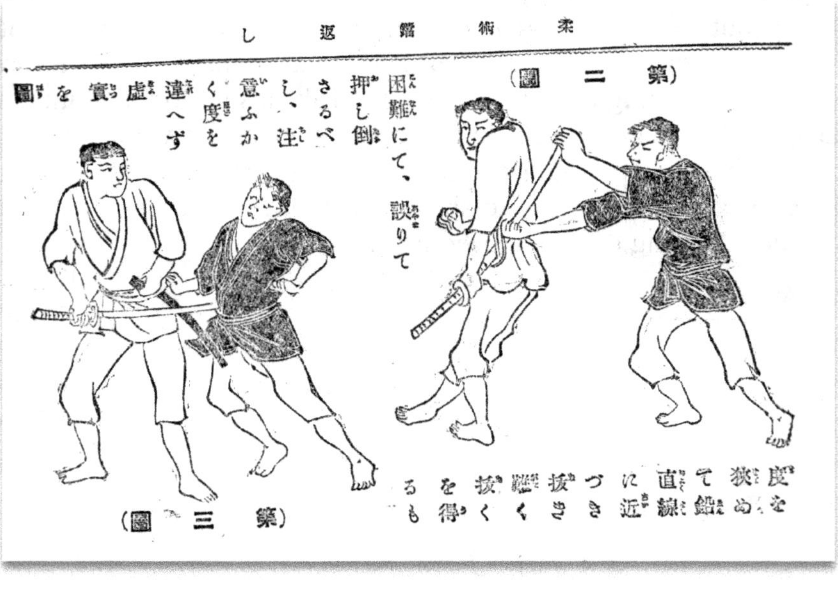

柔 術 鐺 返 し

圖 を 實 虚

圖 三 第

（圖 二 第）

困難にて、誤りて
押し倒
さるべ
し、注
意ふか
く度を
違へず

度を
狹み
て鐺
に近
づき
拔き
拔く
を得
るも

⬤ *Kojiri Kaeshi*
Twisting the End of Your Sword

Illustration 1

Twisting the End of Your Sword is part of Tsuka Sabaki, Seizing the Sword Handle. However, since this technique doesn't involve the handle of your Katana it will be treated as a separate chapter.

As the first illustration shows, you are walking with your sword stuffed in your belt.

Twisting the End of Your Sword

Illustration 1   *Illustration 2*

As the second illustration shows, the Attacker seizes the end of your Katana then twists it while lifting, preventing you from drawing your sword. He will then continue that motion until he shoves you to the ground and finishes you. However, you are on guard and, in the end, the Aattacker is cut down.

This technique begins as shown in the first illustration. You are walking down the street and the Attacker comes running up from behind. He grabs the scabbard of your sword with both hands. He grabs the middle of the scabbard with his right hand and seizes the Kojiri, the ornamental metal cap on the end of the scabbard, with his left hand.

As the second illustration shows he twists your sword up and forward, trying to shove you down.

Twisting the End of Your Sword

Illustration 3

You respond as shown in the third illustration, by drawing your Katana with your right hand and twisting your body counterclockwise before stabbing the attacker in the stomach.

It is important that you do not fail to judge the proper time to draw your sword. If the Attacker is a very strong person he may force the end of your Katana up to a very high angle. Once the scabbard of your sword is nearly vertical it will be very difficult if not impossible to draw. This will likely cause you to fall down.

In order to not get toppled it is essential that you judge the situation carefully and make no mistakes. It is important that you use Kyo-Jitsu, or Deception-Truth, effectively[23]. Look carefully at illustrations two and three

---

[23] Kyo-Jitsu 虚実 is Deception-Reality or Lie and Truth. This means using feints and diversions to conceal your true intent.

家庭内

Katei Nai :

Self-Defense at Home

● *Makura Gatana*
Katana by Your Pillow
Illustration 1

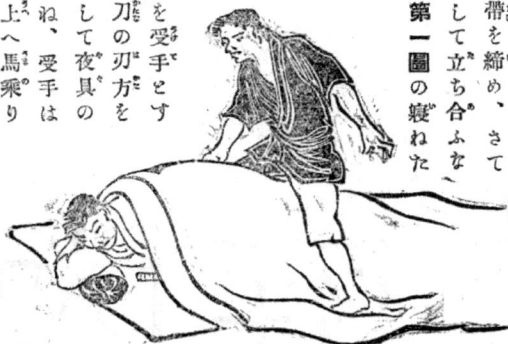

（第　一　圖）

さ忍ひ入り、寝入りたるを害せんとする時、寝たる者眼さめたらば枕元の刀を、おつ取り、何時にても抜けるやう、抜き勝手に、恰も腰に帶したるやう、柄を右上にして下緒を口に啣へ持ち、斯く爲ながらに帶を締め、さて蹈み出して立ち合ふなり。此第一圖の寝たるを使手とし夜具の上に跨りたるを受手とす使手は刀の刃方を向ふにして夜具の中に寝ね、受手は夜具の上へ馬乗りになり、使手の喉を絞めんとするなり、恰も第二圖の如く、刀の両へ旨

二十四　枇柄巻　月

（第　二　圖）

の手を窓にかけ、又、第三圖の如く、夜具の中にて左の手を受手の心付かさるやう、掌を仰向けて受け、激しく跳ね上げて右へ瓢し、第四圖のごとく刀を抜きて挨打ちに斬付くるなり。是等は用心厳しくして刀を夜具の肉に入れて寝ねたるものなれども、年中刀を抱きて寝ねらるゝものにあらず、これは豫曲者の來るを測りたる時なり此受手が使手の喉を締めて縊り殺すならば、目の覚めぬやうに傍らより來りて絞むるなら

Katana by Your Pillow : Illustration 3

三十四　　刀　枕　衛　柔

むにとさくヽ馬乗に（身體を浮けて目の霞
めぬやうにするにもせよ）乗りかゝると云
ふは、使手に心得ありて、油断透間は無
しと思ふが故なり、若し傍らより忍び寄
らば、夜具を投げかけられて擒さるなる
べし、然る故に夜着の上に跨りて、先づ
襟を執り、眉間を打ち
たんと圖るなり、斯
るさき、心
得なくば實
に危ふし、
此形はか
く好き形
なり、常に
此心得ありて、受
手どなり、使手と
なり、捕り合ひて
熟練し置くべきこ
となり、昔しは圖りて襖を以て敷越に禮

（第　三　圖）

Katana by Your Pillow : Illustration 4

衛　防　隱　雪　　四十四

するを首し
めたる事あ
り、此時鐵
扇を敷居の
溝に置き、
発れて
且つ敵
を仕留
めたる
話あり
すべて注意にあ
なり。

●雪隱防衛
これは專ら撃劍に係れるやうなれども、
柔術の手の混りたる所もあり、雪隱の内
より出る者を使手とし、外より窺ひ寄り
て殺さむとする者逆受手とす、因みに云

（第　四　圖）

149

● *Makura Gatana*
Katana by Your Pillow

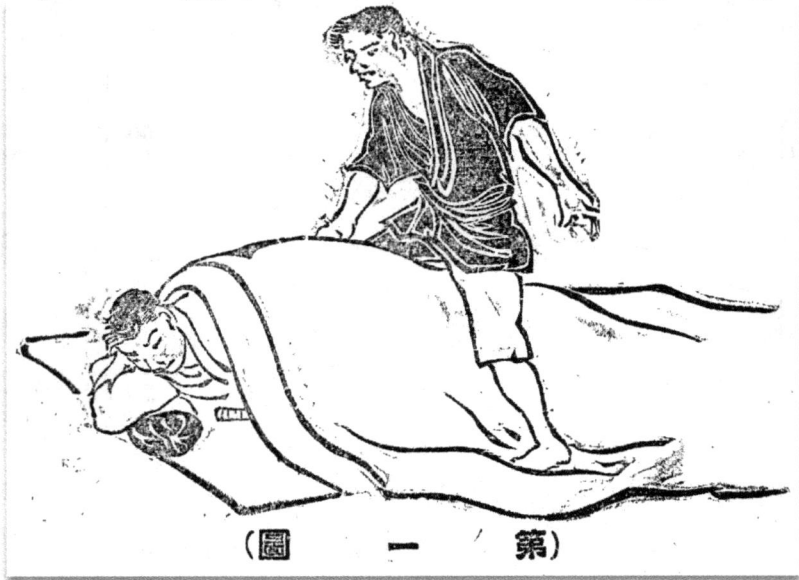

Illustration 1

This is a technique you can use when a Kusemono, "bent person" or villain, sneaks into your house and approaches you while you are asleep. The villain has entered your bedroom and climbed on top of your blankets before squatting down on top of you, with the intention of doing you harm. Fortunately, you have placed your Katana under your blankets. So, after first shoving the villain off, you then do a Nuki-uchi, draw and cut, to eliminate the threat.

Since this is a combination of both Jujitsu and sword fighting, you should understand that it is an application of the skills from both types of martial arts. Long ago, in our country, Samurai would always keep a sword by their pillow in case a thief tried to sneak into their house at night. So, they were prepared to draw at any moment. For them, drawing was automatic. They kept their Katana positioned like it was in their belt with the handle facing up and to the right and holding the Sage-o cord in their mouth. They would simply tighten their belt, then stand and be ready to fight.

Katana by Your Pillow

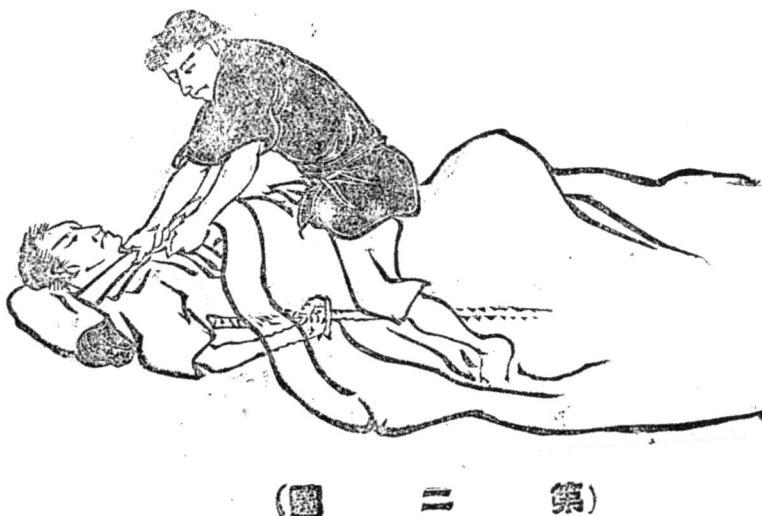

(圖 二 第)

As the first illustration shows, you are asleep and the villain has climbed on top of you and squatted down. However, you have gone to sleep with your sword under your blanket. The blade of your sword is facing away from you. The villain climbs on top of your blankets as if he's mounting a horse and tries to strangle you.

You respond as shown in the second illustration above. Without revealing you are awake, move your right hand to the handle of your sword.

Katana by Your Pillow

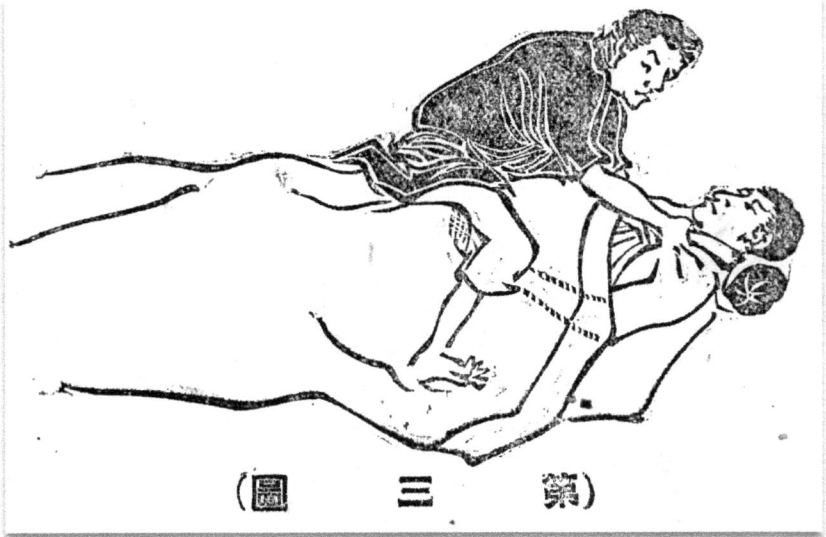

Illustration 3

Next, as the third illustration shows, rotate your left-hand palm up and move it carefully under the blankets so you are holding the man's leg. Do not allow the villain to sense what you are doing. In a sudden violent motion hurl the villain up and to the right so that he flips over.

Katana by Your Pillow

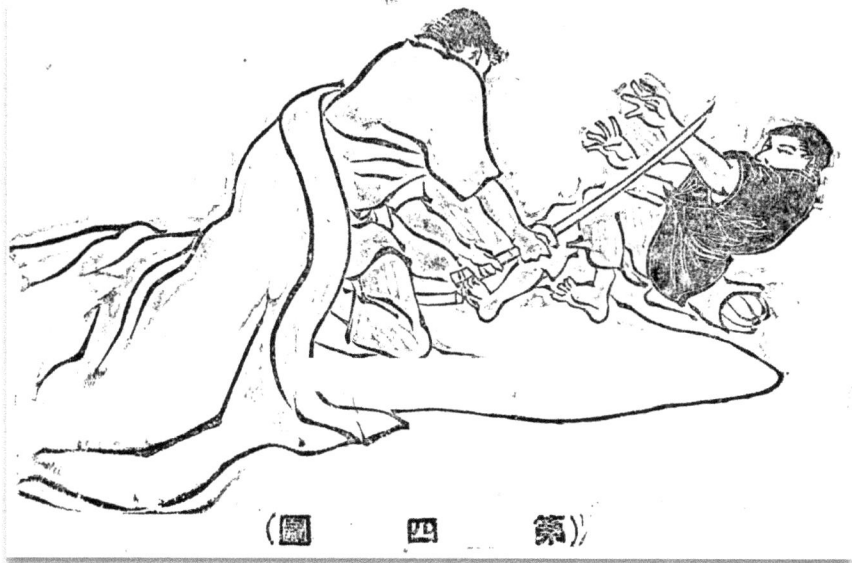

Illustration 4

Then, as Illustration 4 shows, do a Nuki-uchi, drawing and cutting with your Katana in one motion. Only a person who is very careful will sleep with their sword every night. Very few people sleep with their sword every night year-round. In this situation, you suspected a thief or attacker would be targeting you.

Your attacker's goal is to strangle you to death. He approaches from the side and mounts you like he is getting on a horse, then starts to strangle you. (While he is squatting on top of you, he is careful to keep his weight off you in order to prevent you from waking.) However, you are aware of his strategy and have not let your guard down. Another way to handle this situation is to throw your blankets at the villain as he sneaks up on you from the side and capture him in his confusion.

However, in this situation the man has squatted on top of you and taken hold of your collar, readying to strike you in Miken, between the eyebrows. This is clearly a dangerous situation and thus this technique is very useful. You should study it carefully and take it to heart. Train this technique extensively both in the role of the murderer and the person sleeping.

Long ago, I had something similar happen to me. My attacker pushed a standing screen on top of me and then tried to strangle me. Luckily, I had placed a Tessen, iron fan, in the edge of the door and was able to use that to stop my attacker. I was able to avoid disaster because I was careful.

● *Setsuin Boei*
On Guard in the Toilet : Illustration 1

雪　隱　防　衛　四十五

ふ、今は武家の昔し風なければ、雪隱へ脇差を帶て入るここなし、され以前は武家の雪隱は間廣くして疊二疊敷もあり、中に刀掛を置きて刀脇差を掛くるやうにしたり、此捕り方は、使手が、右の第一圖のごとく、脇差を帶して雪隱より出づるを、受手は、傳ひ緣側の、如何にも狹き戶の陰に隱れ居て、左より一打にさ斬り付くるを、使手は素早く脇差を拔きて、此第二圖のご

（第　一　圖）

On Guard in the Toilet : Illustration 2

雪　隱　防　衛　四十六

さく受け止め、同時に受手の刀の柄を左の手にて確かりこ握り、とく少しく體を轉して、腹なりを突くなり。凡そ心がけある人は大抵氣はいに人てあるここを知る。

のなりされば雪隱を出づるさき、豫じめ測算ありて、脇ざしにて右にて柄を握るを期す．此捕り方にては敵の柄を握るここ、第一の働き、卽ち働き

（第　二　圖）

On Guard in the Toilet : Illustration 3

（第　三　圖）

柔　術　坐　捕　　　　七十四

の主なり、何ごとならば、此狭き處にて、奈何にともし難く、故に先づ受け止めたるほ、柄を握らんが爲めなり、廣き所なれば意とせざれども

狭き所故、受手は長き刀の柄を握られて身動きならず、進退自由ならざるうちに腹を突かるゝなり。

◉坐捕

　　　右捕返し

坐捕とは坐りて捕るが故に斯く日ふなり此體は、最初、双方の間を六尺、即ち一間隔て、居合腰に胡坐を組み、両手を両

● *Setsuin Boei*
On Guard in the Toilet

Illustration 1

This technique is considered a sword fighting technique, however there are some elements of Jujutsu mixed in. In this situation you are the person exiting the lavatory and the Attacker is outside the laboratory watching for you to leave so he can kill you.

This scene is one you would find in an old-style Samurai house. Typically, a Samurai would keep his short sword in his belt when entering the lavatory. The lavatory in a typical Samurai household would be about as big as 2 Tatami mats. There would be a Katana-Kake, or sword stand, inside and a Samurai would place his Wakizashi, short sword, on that.

On Guard in the Toilet begins as shown in the first illustration. You are exiting the lavatory with your short sword stuffed into your belt. The Attacker is waiting outside on the connecting veranda. He is hiding in the narrow shadow of the door. He is planning on cutting down your left side.

On Guard in the Toilet

Illustration 2

You respond by rapidly drawing your Kodachi short sword and blocking the Attacker's cut. This is shown in the second illustration. At the same time, seize the handle of his sword with your left hand and hold it firmly.

On Guard in the Toilet

Illustration 3

As the third illustration shows you should then twist your body and stab your Attacker in either the stomach or the armpit.

A true practitioner would, for the most part, be able to sense an Attacker lying in wait. Thus, when exiting the lavatory you have already calculated how your opponent will strike. You will then use the short sword in your right hand to block his cut and then immediately seize the handle of his sword with your left hand.

The first movement you make, which is the focus of this whole technique, requires you to avoid an attack in a small space. Thus, you perform three actions; drawing your short sword, blocking the attack and seizing the handle of his sword. If the space were wider, you would have more options however this technique takes place in a confined space. That is why you grab the handle of the Attacker's sword, so he is no longer able to advance or retreat freely. You then use this opportunity to step in and stab him in the stomach or side.

骨法

Koppo :
Bone Manipulation

● *Meishi Toriho*
Stopping and Arresting a Person
Illustration 1

柔　術　召　捕　法　　二十七

ること肝要なり、右の第二圖、第三圖を見るべし、
●召捕法
召捕法、即ち捕綺法は、柔術の立合科の内にて一に骨法とも云ふ、これも白襦袢に白袴を穿きたる者は使手にて、黑襦袢

に白袴を穿きたる者は受手なり、まれば

（第　一　圖）

Stopping and Arresting a Person : Illustration 2

七十三　　法　捕　召　術　柔

十手を携へたる使手は捕吏にして、受手は罪人に擬するなり、さて初めは六尺へたて、足を外八文字に蹈み、使手は十手を道に持ちて出で（十手は必ず斯く道に持つが法なり、七首を逆に使ふが如し）兩人近よりて使手は十手にて受手の面を打たんこするを、受手は無腰にて何も覆物の無き散り、第二圖

右の腕に之でを受を
、因て使手は第三圖の如く體を左へ轉し、受手の右の二の腕

（第　二　圖）

162

Stopping and Arresting a Person : Illustrations 3 & 4

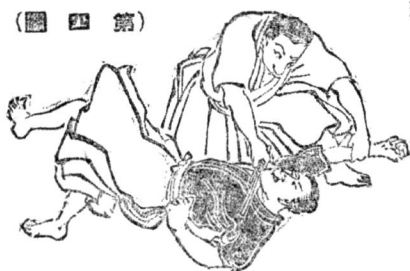

法　捕　召　術　柔　　四十七

（圖四第）

線點し外を足るたけへ、上より左の手を掛けて攫び込み、繋

し、圖ひて
繋かけて左へ倒
を受手の右へ
廻は繋
く、左の足
廻り受手を引き
を示したるが如
にて矢にて方向
擊かけて左へ倒
へ繋け、開さ掛

（圖三第）

● *Meishi Toriho*
Stopping and Arresting a Person

Illustration 1

This technique known as *Stopping and Arresting a Person* is also known as Seizing and Binding. Koppo, or Bone Manipulation, is another name for this. It is a subset of Jujutsu.

In this technique you will be shown in the white shirt and Hakama and the attacker is in the black shirt and Hakama. In addition, since you are the Torie, Arresting Officer, you are carrying a Jutte, Policeman's Truncheon. Your opponent is a person you suspect is a criminal.

Start by standing about 6 Shaku, 180 centimeters apart. You are standing in Soto Hachimonji, or with the toes pointed outward like the bottom of the Kanji for eight 八. You are carrying the Jutte in Saka, a reverse grip. (This school teaches that the Jutte should be initially held in a reverse grip. It is basically the same as when you hold a knife reversed.) [24]

---

[24] Saka, which is short for Saka-te, reverse grip, uses the Kanji 逆 which means "reverse." This means with the metal bar facing down. All brackets are by the author.

Stopping and Arresting a Person

Illustration 2

As you approached the suspect you strike him in the face with your truncheon. Since the suspect is Mugoshi 無腰, has no weapons in his belt, he blocks your attack with his right arm. This is shown in the second illustration.

Stopping and Arresting a Person

Illustration 4 *Illustration 3*

You respond by rotating your body clockwise as you wrap your left arm over the upper part of the suspect's right arm and press in with the Jutte. Sweep out his right foot and rotate counterclockwise a full rotation. This is indicated by the dotted lines and arrow. This action will pull the suspect around.

As the fourth illustration shows, after planting your left foot behind the suspect's right heel you pull him around clockwise and down with a Kakegoe of *Yaa!* You then shoved the end of your Jutte into his throat with a shout of *Un!*

複数相手

Fukusu Aite:
Dealing With Multiple
Opponents

● *Jujutsu Sannin Tori*
Battling Three Opponents Using Jujutsu
Illustration 1

五十七　　捕　人　三　術　柔

手を十にて喉を押ふるなり、

◉柔術三人捕

三人捕は二人捕よりは叉混雜す、故に使手は白襦袢に白股引穿きたる者、受手三人は白襦袢に黒股引穿きたる者甲の受手とし、黒襦袢に白股引穿きたるは乙の受手とし、黒襦袢に黒服引穿きたるは丙の受手とす、又之を畢るは乙の受手ごし

此三人捕の釣り始めは、右の圖に甲受、乙受、丙受と記すべし丙受より使手の胸を執るを、使手は一圖の如く丙受の腕首を執り、第三圖の如く左の手を二次の頁の第二圖のごとく右の手にて丙受の腕首を執り、

（第　1　圖）

Battling Three Opponents Using Jujutsu : Illustration 2

七十六　　捕　人　三　術　柔

右の腕へかけ右の手を持かへ執り上げて右の膝を立て第四圖の如く左へ倒し、鼻と口との間を打つ、是れにて丙は急所を打たれたる事ゆる、のけ反りて絶息す、次で傍に在る乙受は第四圖のごとく使手の後ろ襟を右の手にて執り、後ろへ倒して眉間を打たんごするを、第六圖のごとく使手は倒れながら、右の手

（第　二　圖）

170

Battling Three Opponents Using Jujutsu : Illustration 3

七十七　　　捕　人　三　術　柔

にて受け、受けながら乙受の左の脇を
て、是れをも絶息せしむ、最早甲受一人

第七
圖のごとく
甲受は左の
手にて使手
の衿を執り
右の手にて
睾丸を打たん
とするを、使
手は左の手に
て睾丸を押さ
へ、右の手に
て甲受が、已
れの衿を執り
たる左の手を
受け止め、第

八圖のごとく
甲受を左へ倒
して、左の肱
にて睾丸を中
てるなり。

（第　三　圖）

Battling Three Opponents Using Jujutsu : Illustration 4

捕　人　三　術　柔　　　七十八

是れにて受手は甲乙丙三人とも絶息し、
使手は勝ちを得るなり。さて、第二圖の
所にて使手が丙受の右の腕首を執りたる
手つきを見るべし、斯くも逆に執れり、
是れ執りたる手を外すに便なればなり、
然るに第三圖にては使手が丙受の右の腕
を持つ持ち
方手つき愛
れり、此處
注意ごころ
なり、是れより左
へ倒すれば、右の
手にて敵の腕を逆
に持ちては勝手惡
し、因て左の手
にて上より丙受の
二の腕を持ち、斯
くして右の逆手を
順に持ちかへたる
なり、斯る所は實に細かき注意にして、
順序を誤らずご謂ふべし、又、左へ倒し

（第　四　圖）

171

Battling Three Opponents Using Jujutsu : Illustration 5

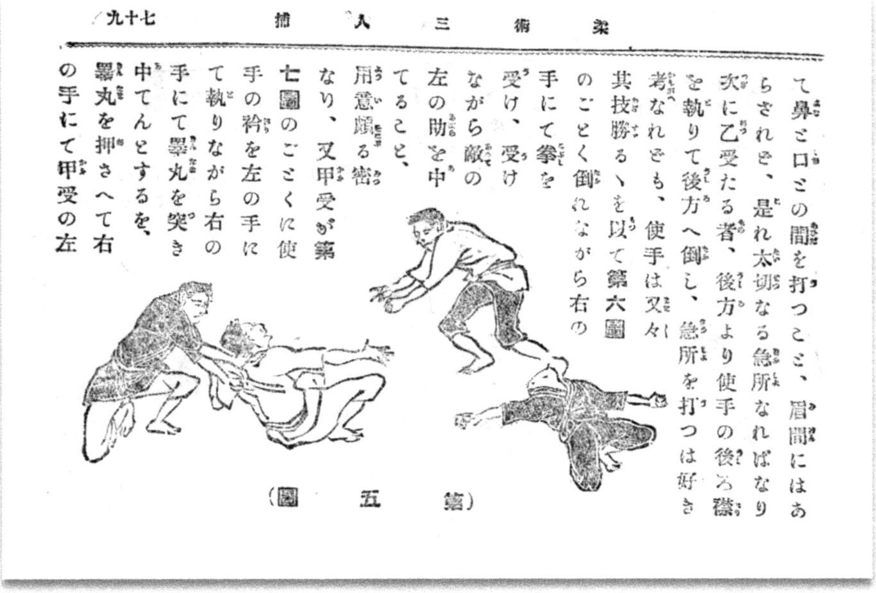
柔術三人捕　七十九

て鼻と口との間を打つこと、眉間にはあらされど、是れ太切なる急所なればなり

次に乙受たる者、後方より使手の後ろ襟を執りて後方へ倒し、急所を打つは好き考なれども、使手は又々其技勝るゝを以て第六圖のごとく倒れながら右の手にて拳を受け、受けながら敵の左の肋を中てること、用意頗る密なり、又甲受が第七圖のごとくに使手の衿を左の手にて執りながら右の手にて睾丸を突き中てんとするを、睾丸を押さへて右の手にて甲受の左

（第五圖）

Battling Three Opponents Using Jujutsu : Illustration 6

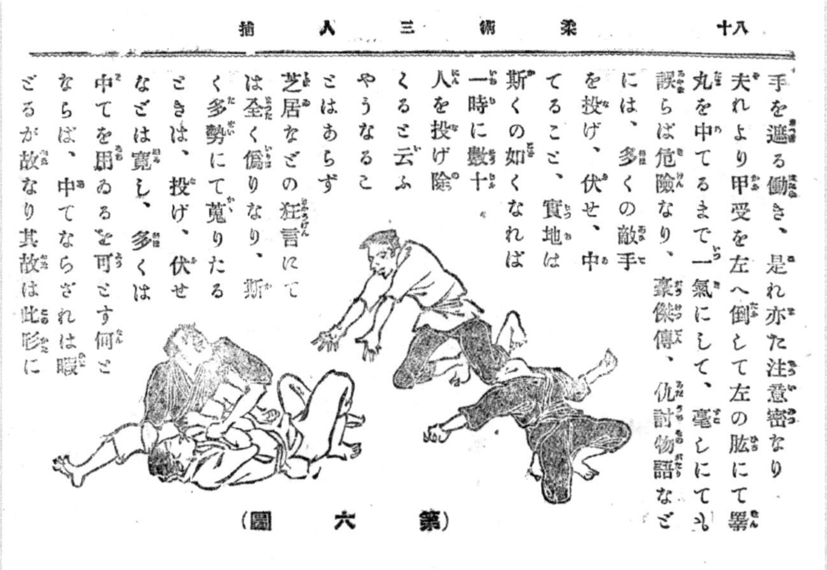
八十　柔術三人捕

手を遮る働き、是れ亦た注意密なり

夫れより甲受を左へ倒して左の肱にて睾丸を中てるまで一氣にして、毫しにても誤らば危險なり、豪傑傳、仇討物語などには、多くの敵手を投げ、伏せ、中てること、實地は斯くの如くなれば一時に數十人を投げ除くると云ふやうなることはあらず芝居などの狂言にては全く偽りなり、斯く多勢にて蒐りたるときは、投げ、伏せなどは寛し、多くは中てを用ゐるを可とす何となれば、中てならざれは暇どるが故なり其故は此形に

（第六圖）

Battling Three Opponents Using Jujutsu : Illustration 7

八十一　　　捕　人　三　術　柔

遭ふやも計れず、高等の術者に遭はば懲
如何なる懲らしめに
れ術は上に上あれば
は甚だ危険なり、是
投げんとするが如き
て酒狂に乗じて人を
少し形を變へたりご
のみ用ゐる術なり、
れ難くて、死するよ
りは術なしと思ふ時
る、如何にしても免
亂暴者に遭ひ、一命に關は
らず、憤んで術を心得、萬一
は遊戯として荷めに思ふべか
必ずしも、徒の体操、或
にて勝負を定むるなり、
てに及ぶまでの、眞似事
には危険なれば、徒た中
然れども此中では、稽古
き鬪にては中てに限るなり。
て受手三人さもに、中てにて殪せり激も

（第　七　圖）

Battling Three Opponents Using Jujutsu : Illustration 8

八十二　　　捕　人　三　術　柔

に易きものより始むべし。
其單簡なる者のうち
單簡なるものあり、
り組みたるものあり
に熱して後とす、又
なるは、一人捕の術
し、二人捕の使手ご
捕の使手さなるに熱
さて此三人捕は二人
然もあらんさ思はる
を記せり、何さま、
達人になるほど、人
を張る、さ云ふここ
るに、武藝は進みて
しの随筆物などを見
居るをよしさす、昔
みて知らざる顔にて
術を知るほど術ほ包
大蔵の因原さ曰へば
出合ふたらば、命をも失ふべし、生兵法
らさるゝまでの事なれども、然なき者に

（第　八　圖）

173

● *Jujutsu Sannin Tori*
Battling Three Opponents Using Jujutsu

Tsukai-te You		
	Hei-uke	*Ko-Uke*

Otsu-Uke

Illustration 1

Clearly battling three opponents is more difficult than battling two. In this technique you are wearing a white top and white pants. You have three opponents, and they are dressed as follows:

Ko-Uke – white shirt black pants
Otsu-Uke – black shirt white pants
Hei-Uke – black shirts black pants

These three will be referred to as the Ko, Otsu and Hei opponents.[25] This technique begins with the Hei-Uke grabbing your chest with his right hand.

---

[25] Ko-Otsu-Hei 甲乙丙 These words are used in Jujutsu instruction manuals to differentiate between opponents when describing a technique. They are also used as grades or ranks similar to A,B,C...However, in this case all the opponents seem to be of equal skill so it is just to differentiate between them. The word Uke means the person receiving the technique.

Battling Three Opponents Using Jujutsu

Illustration 2

You respond as shown in the second illustration. You grab the Hei-uke's wrist with your right hand and shove it off.

Illustration 3

As the third illustration shows, seize the Hei-uke's upper arm with your left hand. Switch the way you are gripping with your right hand and stand up on your right foot. Then throw him down to your left and strike him in in the spot between his mouth and nose. This strike is shown in the fourth illustration.

Battling Three Opponents Using Jujutsu

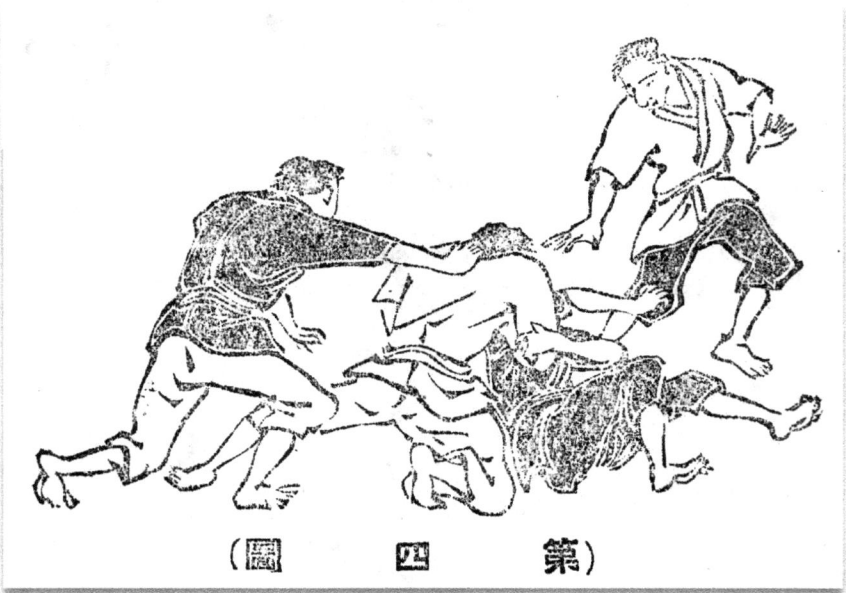

Illustration 4

Since you have thrown the Hei-uke down on his back and struck him in a vital point, he has had the wind knocked out of him. As the illustration above shows the Otsu-Uke then grabs your collar from behind with his right hand.

Battling Three Opponents Using Jujutsu

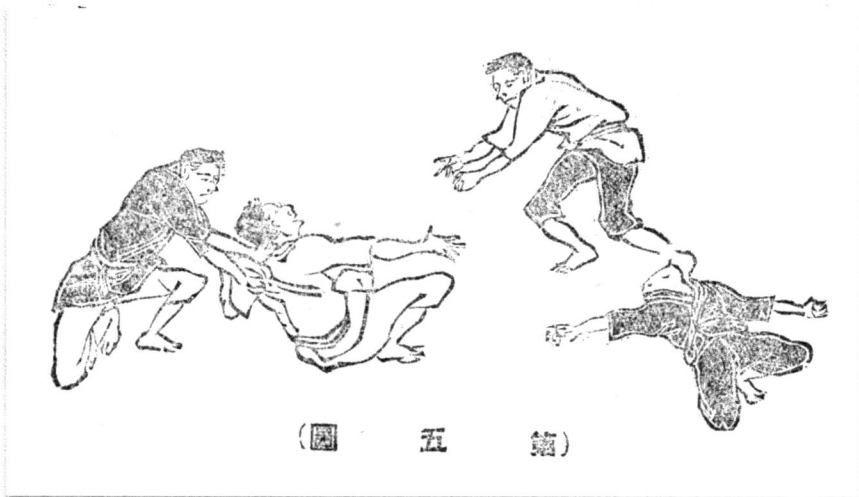

Illustration 5

He yanks you backwards and tries to strike you in Miken, between the eyebrows.

Battling Three Opponents Using Jujutsu

Illustration 6

As the sixth illustration shows you block the Otsu-Uke's punch with your right arm before immediately elbowing him in the ribs. Having been struck in his left ribs, the Otsu-Uke passes out and you are now only facing one attacker, the Ko-Uke.

Illustration 7

The Ko-Uke seizes your collar with his left hand and tries to punch you in the groin with his right fist. Respond by covering your groin with your left hand and use your right arm to knock off the Ko-Uke's hand holding your collar.

Battling Three Opponents Using Jujutsu

Illustration 8

As illustration 8 shows, throw the Ko-Uke to your left and strike him in the groin with your left elbow. With that you have incapacitated all three opponents and are therefore the victor.

Looking back at Illustration 2, carefully note your hand positioning when you seize the Hei-uke's right wrist. Initially you are taking hold of his wrist in a reverse grip, meaning palm up. This makes removing the Attacker's arm easier however in the third illustration you have changed your grip. Pay particular attention to this. Since your next move is toppling him to the left, if you maintain the reverse grip with your right hand toppling him will be difficult to do. So after you grab his upper arm with your left hand switch your right hand from an Gyaku-te, underhand grip, to a Jun-te, overhand grip. While this may seem like a minor detail it is important and is therefore being emphasized.

Illustration 2

Illustration 3

Battling Three Opponents Using Jujutsu

Illustration 5

After switching your grip, throw your opponent down to your left and then strike him in the spot between his nose and his mouth. This is a different spot from Miken, between the eyebrows, however this Kyusho, or vital point, is very important.[26]

Next, you must deal with the Otsu-Uke. He grabs the back of your collar and yanks you to the ground. Now that you are on your back, he hopes to then be able to easily strike you in a vital area.

Illustration 6

Since you have a superior Jujutsu technique you react as shown in the sixth illustration. While lying on your back you block with your right arm. After blocking, immediately strike him in the ribs on his left side with your left elbow. This attack is possible because you are prepared and in control.

---

[26] In many martial arts schools the spot between the upper lip and the nose is called Jinchu 人中 "center of man."

Battling Three Opponents Using Jujutsu

Illustration 7

Finally, the Ko-Uke seizes your collar with his left hand and tries to strike you in the groin with his right fist. This is shown in the seventh illustration. You respond by covering your groin with your left hand and using your right arm to sweep away your opponent's left hand which is gripping your collar. Pay close attention to how this action is done.

Illustration 8

Then in one quick movement you topple the Ko-Uke to the left and drop your left elbow into his groin. If you make even the slightest error here it will put you in great danger.

Tales of famous Samurai swordsman and stories of revenge often contain scenes where the hero throws, pins or strikes multiple opponents. In reality, throwing a dozen attackers is only found in theater or comical storytelling.

In other words, it is completely fictional. When fighting a large group of attackers, you are better off eschewing throws and pins and instead rely on striking. If you are not striking, then it means you have time on your hands. That is what this technique is showing. You are in an intense fight with three adversaries, and you defeated them by relying on violent strikes.

◉ *Gekken Jujutsu Ninin Tori: Dai-ichi Kata*
Dealing With Two Opponents Using Gekken & Jujutsu
Kata #1
Illustration 1

◎撃剣柔術二人捕　第一形

二人捕とは使手一人に受手二人の蒐る捕方を云ふ、斯の如く受手は二人あるが故に説明甚だ入り組めば、一人を甲の受手、一人を乙の受とし甲受、乙受と省略して記すべし、さて又、着類にても一目して分別せしめんが為に、白の襦袢を着て黒の袴を穿きたる者を甲受とし、黒の襦袢に白の袴を穿きたる者を乙受と定む、白き襦袢に白の袴は使手なり

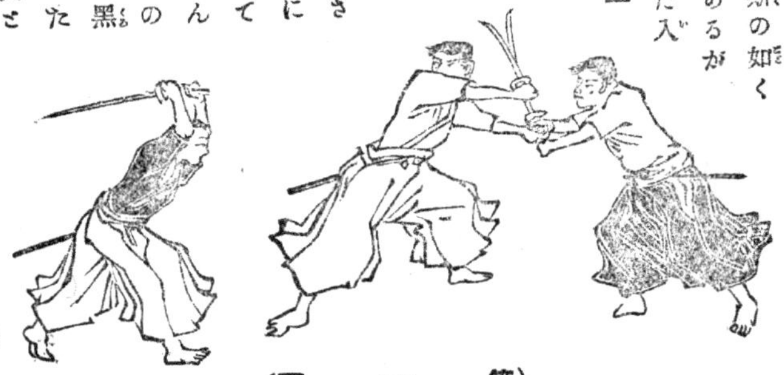

(第一圖)

Illustration 2

さて乙受が刀を抜きて第一圖のごとく使手に斬て蒐るを使手は抜き合せて受け流し、甲受も亦た使手目がけて第二圖の如く斬かゝるが故に乙受の刀を受けながし、甲受の刀を神速に受く、乙受復た斬り付けて第三圖の如く遂に使手の刀を打落す此時甲受は傍らに在りて使手の透を見る。

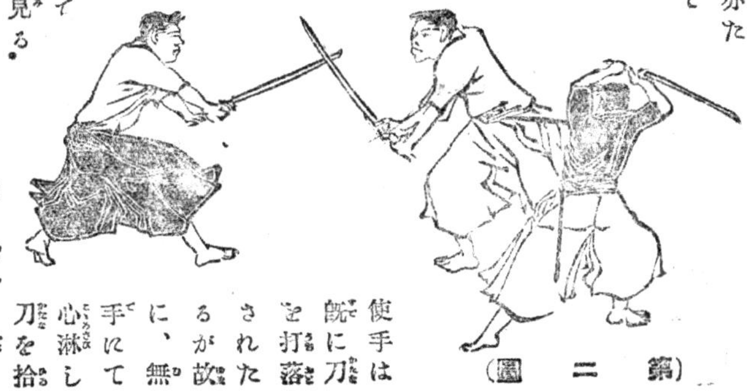

(第二圖)

使手は既に刀を打落されたるが故に、無手にて心淋し刀を拾はんとすれども、二人の敵は抜身を構へて鋭く迫り、其れを拾はむ透間も無けれ

Illustration 3

擊劔柔術二人捕　六十

ば、止むなく、劔術の手にて第四圖の如く乙受の衿を左の手にて執り、右の手にて二の腕を受け、左の足を繋けて、第五圖のごとく投げ、第四圖のごとく刀をふり翳して來る甲受を左の手の肱にて第六圖の如く中て、悶絕せしむ、乙受は之を見て、拔刀を以て使手の眉間を突かんとし、起き上り來ると、第七圖の如く右の手にて衿を執り、左の手にて右腕を執り、第八圖のごとく向ふへ投げて、右の手の拳にて

（第　三　圖）

Illustration 4

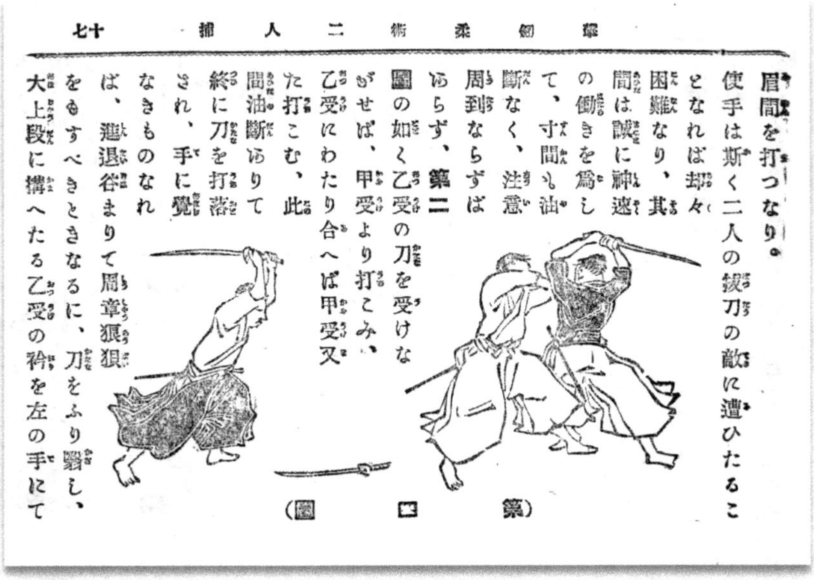

擊劔柔術二人捕　七十

眉間を打つなり。使手は斯く二人の拔刀の敵に遭ひたることなれば却々困難なり、其間は誠に神速の働きを爲して、寸間も油斷なく、注意周到ならずばあらず、第二圖の如く乙受の刀を受けながせば、甲受より打こみ、乙受にわたり合へば甲受又た打こむ、此間油斷ありて終に刀を打落され、手に覺なきものなればば、逡巡谷まりて周章狼狽をなすべきときなるに、刀をふり翳し、大上段に構へたる乙受の衿を左の手にて

（第　四　圖）

Illustration 5

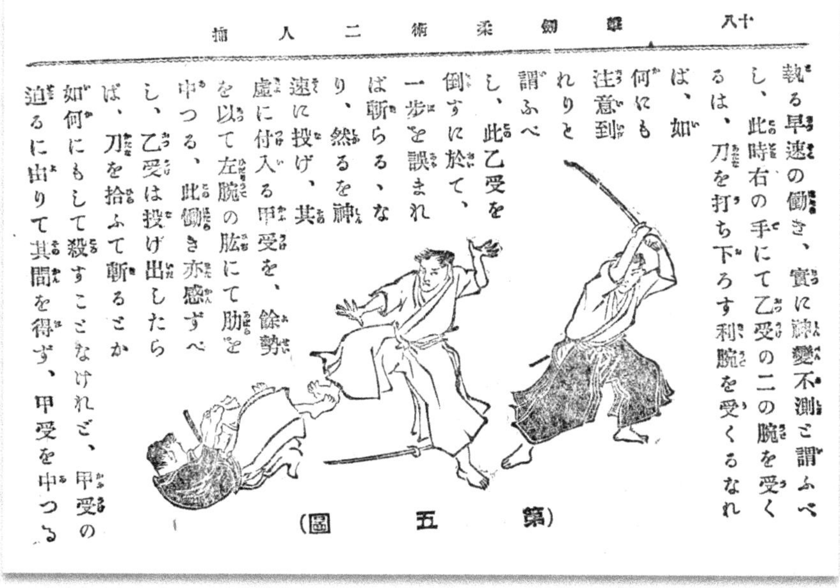

擊劍柔術二人捕　十八

載る早速の働き、實に臨變不測と謂ふべ
し、此時右の手にて乙受の二の腕を受く
るは、刀を打ち下ろす利腕を受くるなれ
ば、如何にも注意到れりと謂ふべ
し、此乙受を倒すに於て、一歩を誤まれ
ば、斬らる、なり、然るを神速に投げ、其
處に付入る甲受を、餘勢を以て左腕の脇にて脇を
中つる、此働き亦感ずし、乙受は投げ出したら
ば、刀を拾ふて斬るさか如何にもして殺すことなけれど、甲受の
迫るに出りて其間を得ず、甲受を中つる

(第　五　圖)

Illustration 6

擊劍柔術二人捕　十九

虚を見て乙受は起き上り、起き上りさま
し、使手の鬱丸を突かんこするは早速の心が
け妙なり、然れども使手は透かさず右の
手にて胸を執り、左の手
にて右腕を執る
は妙手なり。
又、投げて眉間を
打つに、乙受の刀
を持ちたる脇を執
りて自由ならせ
るは心得ある者の
働きなり、昔時武者修
行なごにて諸國を巡る
勇士は、多數の敵を事
こもせず、取ては投げ
〳〵、人礫を打ちて、人
體を以て人を打ち倒〳〵たりなご言ふもの
あれど、實際然ることのあるものならず

(第　六　圖)

Illustration 7

大抵俠倆は、大して懸隔あるものにあらず、多數の敵を相手にするは隨分骨の折るゝものなり、手に覺へあり、體坐れば畏るゝにも及ばざれども。

さりとて侮るべからず敵は強きものは思ひ居るべし或人往年住吉御道を、深夜十二時を過ぎて一時二時とも思しき頃、堺より大坂へ車に乗りて歸りしに、天下茶屋近くなり吉と經過ぎ、舊刑塲跡なる薦田の邊にて、怪しの男、人力車を引はさみ、「オイく、些と無心が有るから下りろ」と呼はり、車上の

（第七圖）

飽に拔刀にて二人の賊は迫れり、

Illustration 8

人は手に覺へある人なれども、車上にては奈何ともすること能はず、是は困つた事ぞと思ふうちに、車夫は最早何處へ行きけん、慄れて遍げ行傍へにも在らず、因て殊に弱き者に裝ひ、故ぞ、瓦駄くと震ふに對ひ、「諾ーい、何とも賊二人さまを爲して、何卒命ばかりは御助け下され、決して手向ひなどは致す覺へも無い者です」と慄れ入るさまを見せければ、二人の賊は横柄に「下りないか、何を愚圖く！曰ふ、身ぐるみに脱いで所持の物を皆渡せば可いサア速く下りろ」と、益々迫る、其人は沈着はらつて、「下りまするが僕は、此節淋病で、

（第八圖）

Illustration 8.1

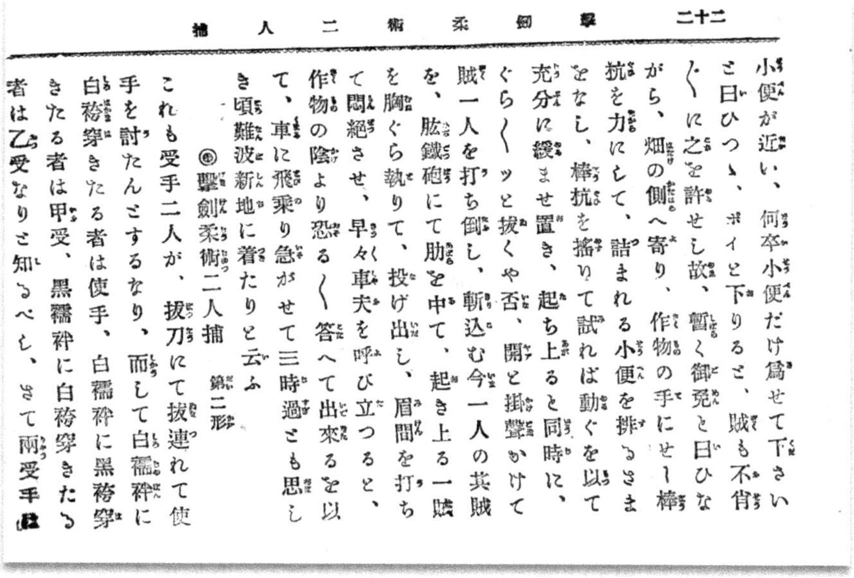

二十二　挙御　柔術　二人捕

小便が近い、何卒小便だけ爲せて下さいと曰ひつゝ、ボイと下りるさ、賊も不肖くに之を許せし故、暫く御免と曰ひながら、畑の側へ寄り、作物の手にせし棒抗を力にして、詰まれる小便を排らさまとなし、棒抗を搖りて試れば動ぐを以て充分に緩ませ置き、起ち上ると同時に、ぐらぐらッと拔くや否、開と掛聲かけて賊一人を打ち倒し、斬込む今一人の其賊を、肱鐵砲にて肋を中て、起き上る一睨を胸ぐら執りて、投げ出し、眉間を打ちて悶絶させ、早々車夫を呼び立つると、作物の陰より恐るゝ答へて出來るを以て、車に飛乗り急がせて三時過さも思しき頃難波新地に着たりと云ふ

◉擊劍柔術二人捕
第二形

これも受手二人が、拔刀にて拔連れて使手を討たんさするなり、而して白襦袢に白袴穿きたる者は使手、白襦袢に黑袴穿きたる者は甲受、黑襦袢に白袴穿きたる者は乙受なりさ知るべし、さて兩受手は

● *Gekken Jujutsu Ninin Tori: Dai-ichi Kata*
Dealing With Two Opponents Using Gekken & Jujutsu
Kata #1

Illustration 1

The meaning of *Dealing With Two Opponents Using Gekken & Jujutsu* is that you have two opponents, armed with swords, who are attacking you at the same time. Since this will describe both how your attackers cut with their swords, as well as how you respond to this double-attack, the explanation is somewhat complicated. The attackers will be referred to as the Ko-Uke, former attacker, and Otsu-Uke, latter attacker. For simplicity's sake they will be referred to as Ko-Uke and Otsu-Uke.

To make identifying the combatants easier, their clothing will be differentiated. The attacker wearing a white shirt and a black Hakama skirt will be the Ko-Uke while the attacker wearing a black shirt and white Hakama will be the Otsu-Uke. You will be dressed in a white shirt and white Hakama.

The technique begins as shown in the first illustration. The Otsu-Uke draws his Katana and cuts. You quickly draw your sword and block his attack allowing his sword to slide off your blade. At the same time the Ko-Uke is preparing to attack you.

Dealing With Two Opponents Using Gekken & Jujutsu Kata #1

Illustration 2

As the second illustration shows, after blocking the Otsu-Uke's attack and allowing his sword cut to slide off your sword, you then turn to deal with the Ko-Uke. In a rapid movement you block the Ko-Uke's attack. At this point the Otsu-Uke is preparing to cut again.

Dealing With Two Opponents Using Gekken & Jujutsu Kata #1

Illustration 3

As the third illustration shows the Otsu-Uke strikes your sword hard enough to cause you to drop it.

The Ko-Uke, who is off to your side, sees that you are now open. Since your sword has been knocked from your hands you are now unarmed and in a perilous position. You attempt to retrieve your sword however as your opponents already have their swords drawn and are advancing quickly, you do not have any time. Since you have no sword, you will have to rely on Jujutsu.

Dealing With Two Opponents Using Gekken & Jujutsu Kata #1

Illustration 4

As the fourth illustration shows you grab Otsu-Uke's collar with your left hand and grab his upper arm with your right hand.

Dealing With Two Opponents Using Gekken & Jujutsu Kata #1

Illustration 5

Plant your left foot behind his left leg and, as shown in the fifth illustration throw him down.

The Ko-Uke raised his sword in the previous fourth illustration, and now he is advancing on you.

Dealing With Two Opponents Using Gekken & Jujutsu Kata #1

Illustration 6

As the sixth illustration shows, you strike the Ko-Uke with your left elbow, thereby knocking him unconscious. The Otsu-Uke, who has been watching this recovers his fighting spirit, stands and attempts to stab you in the groin with his sword.

Dealing With Two Opponents Using Gekken & Jujutsu Kata #1

Illustration 7

As the seventh illustration shows grab the Otsu-Uke's collar with your right hand and his right arm with your left.

Dealing With Two Opponents Using Gekken & Jujutsu Kata #1

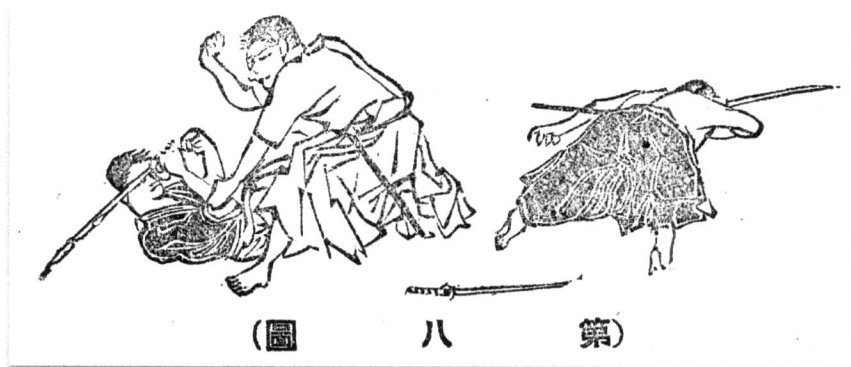

Illustration 8

As the eighth illustration shows, throw him backwards and then punch to Miken, between his eyebrows, with your right fist.

Encountering two opponents who draw swords and attack is a difficult situation indeed. Dueling with them is going to require that you move extremely fast and maintain awareness of everything around you. This is an essential point.

Dealing With Two Opponents Using Gekken & Jujutsu Kata #1

Illustration 2   *Illustration 3*

As the second illustration shows the Otsu-Uke has cut with his Katana. Just as you block and pass this attack the Ko-Uke cuts at you. Thus, having dealt with the Otsu-Uke's attack you have to immediately respond to the Ko-Uke's attack.

However, though you have maintained your vigilance, in the end, as shown in Illustration 3, your Katana is knocked from your hands. You are now in an extreme situation where you must decide whether to advance or retreat, and both choices are fraught with danger.

Illustration 4   *Illustration 5*

The Otsu-Uke has brought his sword high above his head in O-jodan stance and is preparing to cut down. You respond by moving towards him rapidly and seizing his collar with your left hand and his upper arm with you right. Note that this movement must be completely unpredictable and catch your opponent off-guard.

The reason you use your right hand to seize the Otsu-Uke's upper arm is because that is the arm that's putting the most power into the cut. It goes without saying all these points need to be studied very carefully since if you make one mistake while trying to topple the Otsu-Uke, you will be cut down.

However, you throw him down rapidly and with great force. From the Ko-Uke's perspective it looks like you are vulnerable however this is a feint, and you use your use the energy left over from your throw to drive your left elbow into his ribs. Try to visualize this movement.

After throwing the Otsu-Uke, since the Ko-Uke is charging at you, there is no time to retrieve your sword, as you would surely be cut down in the process of picking it up

Illustration 6   *Illustration 7*

The Otsu-Uke, who is recovering, has seen you set up the Ko-Uke and then strike him with your elbow. As the Otsu-Uke rises, he attempts to stab you in the groin.

Illustration 8

This is a clever attack and would usually succeed, however you were able to see his intent and use your right hand to grab his chest. With your left hand you grab his right arm in a quick movement. After throwing him down you then strike him in Miken, between his eyebrows. It is important to note that when you take hold of the Ko-Uke's elbow, you deprive him of his freedom of movement.

Long ago, Samurai would travel around all the regions of Japan to train and duel with other famous warriors to increase their skill. You often hear that these Samurai would take on multiple opponents and handle them without much trouble. They would throw them about and knock them aside as if they were pebbles, even going so far as to throw one person into another person. In reality this did not happen.

One reason is that, for the most part, these men were equally matched so therefore taking on many opponents who are of equivalent skill would likely leave you with many broken bones.

When training you must have confidence in yourself, if you focus your energy you will not become fearful, however do not become hateful. Let the opponent think he is strong.

A few years back a certain person was travelling down the Sumiyoshikaido, a road that connects Osaka to Sakai. It was late at night, well past midnight and probably closer to 1 or 2 am. The man was traveling home from Sakai to Osaka by rickshaw. He had already passed by the Sumiyoshi Grand Shinto Shrine and was in the vicinity of the Hida former execution grounds in the Tengachaya "Heavenly Tea House" neighborhood. Suddenly a suspicious sounding voice called the rickshaw driver to stop. The voice then said, "Hey there! I have a small matter I wish to discuss with you please get out of the cart."

The man in the rickshaw then watched as not one but two highwaymen with swords drawn appear out of the shadows. As it turned out the man riding in the rickshaw was a man confident in his abilities. However, since he was seated inside a rickshaw, he wasn't sure how to solve this situation and he thought he might have a difficult time. Meanwhile the driver of the rickshaw had been so scared he thought only of fleeing the situation and had scampered off somewhere.

The veteran practitioner of Jujutsu and Gekken decided he would pretend to be frightened and weak, so he made it seem as if he was shaking with fear. Addressing the two highwaymen the veteran said in a querulous voice, "I understand, I understand I'll give you everything I have please just leave me with my life! I'm begging you I have no way to defend myself!" Continuing in this fashion the two thieves scoffed at him and increased the pressure. "Climb down out of there and stop wasting our time! Empty your pockets and hand over everything! You hear me?! Hurry up let's get on with it!"

While the veteran appeared outwardly nervous, on the inside he remained calm. "I'm coming down right now!" he said, "But please, I have a weak bladder and it means I have to urinate frequently, please just let me go to the bathroom for a moment!"

As the veteran said this he clambered out of the rickshaw and with the highwaymen's grudging agreement he walked over to the side of the road. There was a rice field adjacent to the road and the veteran placed his hand on a fence pole as he squatted down pretending he needed to use the pole to keep his balance. He tested the pole and found it was somewhat loose. While making actions that would seem like he was urinating he covertly worked the pole back and forth. Pretending to be finished, he stood up. As he did so. he gave the pole a final yank, pulling it free. With a shout of *Yaa!* he charged the first highwayman and struck him down. The second robber was already attacking and the veteran hit him in the ribs with a Hiji-Teppo, an elbow strike as hard as a matchlock shot. The first highwayman was finally getting up and advancing again. The veteran grabbed his chest and threw him down before striking him between the eyebrows knocking him unconscious.

He called out for the rickshaw driver who answered while creeping out of the shadows still consumed with fear. The veteran seated himself in the rickshaw and commanded the driver to begin at a fast pace. They set off and he probably arrived home in the New Town section of Namba, Osaka at around 3:00 o'clock in the morning.

● *Gekken Jujutsu Ninin Tori: Dai-ni Kata*
Dealing With Two Opponents Using Gekken & Jujutsu Kata #2

撃剣柔術二人捕　二十二

小便が近い、何卒小便だけ為せて下さい
さ曰ひつゝ、ポイと下りるさ、賊も不肖
くゝに之を許せし故、暫く御兔と曰ひな
がら、畑の側へ寄り、作物の手にせ一棒
杭を力にして、詰まれる小便を排らさま
となし、棒杭を揺りて試れば動くを以て
充分に緩ませ置き、起ち上ると同時に、
賊一人を打ち倒し、斬込む今一人の其賊
を、脇鐵砲にて脇を中て、起き上る一賊
を胸ぐら執りて、投げ出し、眉間を打ち
て悶絶させ、早々車夫を呼び立つると、
作物の陰より恐ろ〳〵答へて出來るを以
て、車に飛乗り急がせて三時過ぎも思し
き頃難波新地に着きたりと云ふ

●撃剣柔術二人捕
　　　　第二形
これも受手二人が、拔刀にて拔連れて使
手を討たんさするなり、而して白襦袢に
白襦袢きたる者は使手、白襦袢に黑袴穿
きたる者は甲受、黑襦袢に白袴穿きたる
者は乙受なりさ知るべし、さて両受手は

Dealing With Two Opponents Using Gekken & Jujutsu #2
Illustration 1

撃剣柔術二人捕　二十三

拔き連れて使手に、此第一圖の如くに斬
り寛るを、使手は受けて流し第二圖のご
さく甲受が持ちたる刀の
柄を左の手にて執り
神速に第三圖の如
く甲受の横腹を突
き、突きながら乙
受の迫り來るを顧
み、第四圖のごと
く乙受の更に
來るを第五圖
にふりかざし
兩手にて上段
のごとく使手
は左の手にて乙受
の右の手の脇を持
ちて刀を下ろさせ
ず、第六圖のごとく
乙受の腕を持ちながら
刀を持ちたる右の手にて
其後ろ袴を持ち、後ろへ廻りて、開こ聲

（圖　一　第）

Dealing With Two Opponents Using Gekken & Jujutsu #2
Illustration 2

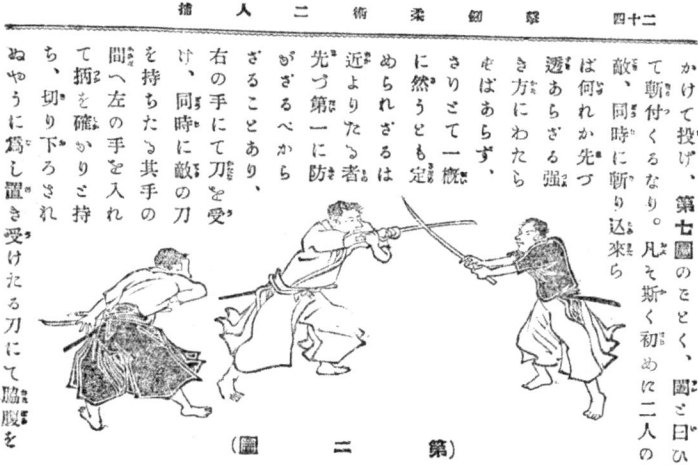

Dealing With Two Opponents Using Gekken & Jujutsu #2
Illustration 3

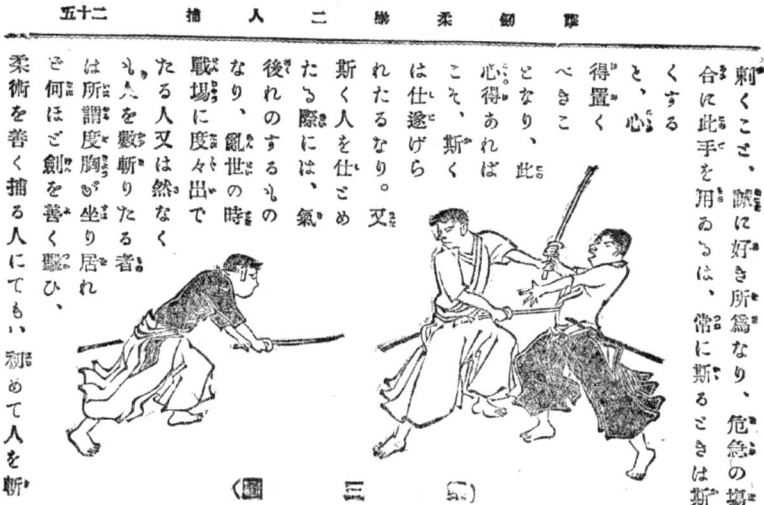

Dealing With Two Opponents Using Gekken & Jujutsu #2

Illustration 4

撃劔柔術二人捕　　二十六

俟ほ迫り來りて斬りかくるなれば、氣後れせざること肝要なり、又此第五圖のごとく、上段に構へて両手にて斬り、右の片腕を止むるとも、左手のみにて斬り附くることあり、因て敵の後ろ衿を執るまで、又執りて投ぐるま、〻投げて斬るまで、少しも氣に間隙あるべからず、開と

りたるときには、唇は紫色と為り、瞬時は泛然さしてそみ居るやうの事あり、此形などは、一人は仕留めたれど〻一人

Dealing With Two Opponents Using Gekken & Jujutsu #2
Illustration 5

撃劔柔術二人捕　　二十七

掛聲をかけたらば、闘と曰ふまでは一氣にすべし、何分にも神速ならざれば目的を達することを能はさるなり、又、此際に、刀を持ちながら敵の後ろ衿を執るは、平生其執り方に慣れ置かずばあらず、又、執れば體を後ろへ廻はして腰に掛くるといふ事も、一部分づ〻慣れ置くべきことなり、次の第六圖の敵の腕を持ちたる手つき、又、刀を持ちながら衿を執りたる手つき、腰の矩合、足つきの矩合、萬端に眼を着けて味ふべし、斯るさざは餘ほど

Dealing With Two Opponents Using Gekken & Jujutsu #2

Illustration 6

擊劍柔術二人捕　二十八

熟せずは為し能はず、返すぐ〜も平常手
練あるべき事なり、此形も亦人深夜に他
より歸るとき、折ふし月夜なりしが陰な
る家かげに
添ひて、
賊二人從
き來り、
淋しき處
にて顯れ
て、斬て蒐りた
ちに賊は拔れ
句は無くて、直
例のおざし文
るを、粗ば此形
にて二人とも仕
留めたりと云ふ
此第二圖の敵の
刀を受けて、同
時に敵の刀の柄
を確かりと執るは、室内の狹き處にて
長物にて斬り付けんとするを受け止めて

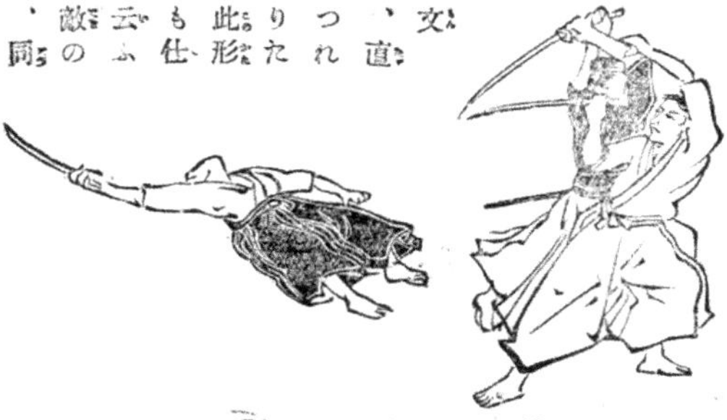

（第　六　圖）

Dealing With Two Opponents Using Gekken & Jujutsu #2
Illustration 7

二十九　捕人二術柔劍擊

此形に由るは誠によし、
柔術は殊に機轉なり
其場によりて臨機
應變の手を出さ
んと思はべ數
多く形を覺へ
置くに如くは
無し、數知り
置きて時に其
宜しきを出す
べし、さて、
二人づりの刀
の分は此二本
さして、次に
は鎗と、刀に
係るさを示すべし。

◎劍鎗柔術二人捕　第一形

劍は關口流にして、槍は大嶋流なり、此
第一圖は禮式の体を示すなり、何れも體
古槍の穗を左にして體す、これも左の白
繻袢白袴は使手にして、右の白繻袢黑袴は

（第　七　圖）

● *Gekken Jujutsu Ninin Tori: Dai-ni Kata*
Dealing With Two Opponents Using Gekken & Jujutsu Kata #2

Otsu-Uke

Tsukai-te
You

Ko-Uke

Illustration 1

This technique also consists of two opponents drawing their swords and attacking you. You will be shown in a white shirt and white Hakama. The Ko-Uke is shown in a white shirt and black Hakama. The Otsu-Uke is shown wearing a black shirt and a white Hakama.

As the first illustration shows your two attackers are advancing with swords drawn readying to cut you down.

Dealing With Two Opponents Using Gekken & Jujutsu Kata #2

Illustration 2

As the second illustration shows you block the Ko-Uke's attack with your sword allowing the energy of his Katana to slide down your blade.[27]

Illustration 3

After blocking the Ko-Uke's cut, move in and grab the handle of his sword with your left hand. Use the sword in your right hand stab the Ko-Uke's in his right side. As you do this be aware that the Otsu-Uke is advancing rapidly.

---

[27] The Ko-Uke's shirt changes from white to black in Illustration 2 and then back to white in illustration 3.

Dealing With Two Opponents Using Gekken & Jujutsu Kata #2

Illustration 4

As the fourth illustration shows, the Otsu-Uke is charging towards you with his sword raised high overhead in a two-handed grip. He is ready to cut down.

Illustration 5

As the fifth illustration shows reach out with your left hand and seize the Otsu-Uke's right elbow. This will prevent him from cutting down with his Katana.

Dealing With Two Opponents Using Gekken & Jujutsu Kata #2

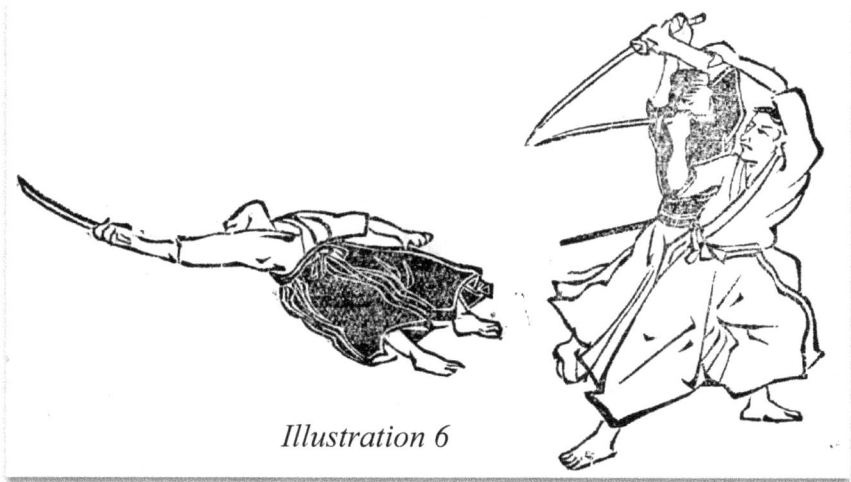

Illustration 6

As the sixth illustration shows you continue to hold his right arm with your left hand. Grab the back of his collar with your right hand while still holding your sword.

Illustration 7

Next, rotate behind your opponent and, with a Kake-goe shout of *Yaa!* throw him down. This is shown in the seventh illustration. After you throw him down, cut him with a shout of *Un!*

In this situation, two people are cutting at you at the same time. Some people say that you must take on the strongest fighter first, since he is the one who is least likely to have an opening in his defenses. However, while not a rule, I believe it is best to defend against the opponent that is closest.

Illustration 2   *Illustration 3*

Focus your power in your right hand as you block the Ko-Uke's cut. As soon as you block, seize the handle of his Katana with your left hand. You should grab the handle between his hands. This will prevent him from cutting down with his sword. Then, after blocking his attack, stab him in the side with your sword.

This is truly an important point in this technique, and it requires a lot of deftness. If you wish to use this technique in an extreme situation, then you need to regularly train it as shown and memorize all the steps. If you follow the instructions as shown and learn them, you will succeed in such a situation.

An important lesson to remember is when you cut a person down it is easy to become distracted. In the Warring States period (1467~1615) a veteran warrior who had experience on the battlefield would be able to cut down many people without it affecting his mental state. We would say such a person is steadfast because he attacks skillfully with his sword and is able to capture people with his Jujutsu quite easily.

However, when you cut a person down for the first time your lips will turn purple, and you will stand there swaying in shock. In this technique, after you have cut down the first attacker, the second attacker is closing in on you. Since he too is seeking to cut you down, it is essential that you do not delay after your first attack.

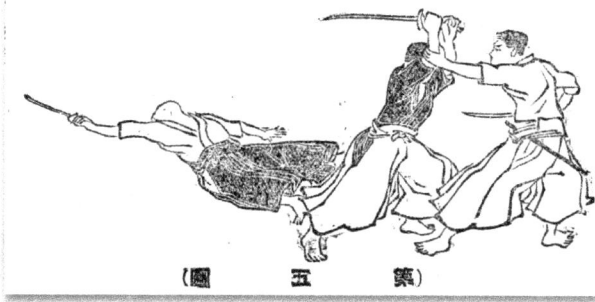

Illustration 5

As the fifth illustration shows, the second attacker is advancing while holding his sword high over his head, readying to cut down on you with both hands. Respond by stopping his right elbow with your left hand, which means your attacker can only use his left arm to cut. It is essential that you do not allow your concentration to lapse in this crucial moment. Next, move in and grab the back of his collar with your right hand. Finally, throw him down and cut.

This whole sequence should be done with intense marital energy. Your shout should begin with the initial block with your left hand and continue as you grab his collar and throw. Your shout continues throughout this continuous motion and ends when you cut.

If every point of this technique is not the done as described

above, you will not be able to effectively achieve your goal. Note that being able to grab the back of an opponent's collar while holding your sword at the same time requires a lot of practice. Without extensive, regular training you will not be able to perform this part of the technique. In addition, you also need to practice moving your body around behind your opponent and placing your hips correctly. Each part of this technique requires practice.

Illustration 6 (left) shows how you should hold the opponent's arm. Consider carefully how your hand is positioned as you grip the back of his collar while, at the same time, holding onto your sword. Also the position of your hips, the position of your feet and every other important detail should be scrutinized.

All these aspects need to be trained extensively or you will not be able to execute them proficiently. These techniques should be included in your training regimen.

This technique was developed because a certain person I know had an encounter one night. He was walking down an alley between two rows of houses. Though the moon was out the shadows were deep. In a lonely spot two thieves suddenly appeared. Unlike in the situation with the rickshaw, they didn't say anything, but just advanced with swords drawn, seemingly intent on killing. My friend used the technique *Dealing With Two Opponents Using Gekken & Jujutsu* to put an end to the two thieves who attacked him.

Illustration 2   *Illustration 3*

Returning to Illustrations 2 & 3, after blocking the first attacker's cut, note how you immediately seize the handle of his sword. This type of action can also be used when battling in confined spaces such as inside a room or against long weapons. This technique is extremely effective in stopping such attacks.

Jujutsu requires that you respond to the situation at hand. Remember the saying *Rin-Ki-Oh-Hen*, "adapting your strategy to the requirements of the moment." It is not necessary to memorize a great number of techniques, rather it is more important that you apply the technique that best matches the situation at hand.

This ends the introduction of techniques dealing with battling two opponents armed with swords. The next section will look at situations involving a combination of spear fighting and sword fighting.

● *Ken-So Jujutsu Futari Tori: Dai-Ichi Kata*
Battling Two Opponents Using Spear, Sword & Jujutsu #1
Illustration 1

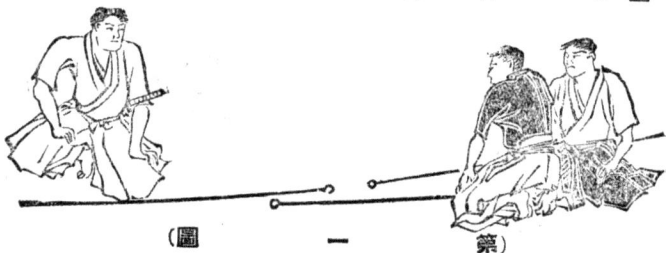

思ひ、双方が搆へ
んとし、使手も突
びて、使手を突か
く受手甲乙二人並
立ち上り、圖の如
二圖は、體終りて
突くべし、さて此第
かず、すり込みて
突くときも、徒突
つべからざ、又、
所まで、詰めて持
つなり、石づきの
き三寸を餘して持
槍の作法は、石づ
合ふこさなるが、
は立ち上りて突き
なり、さて第二圖
粋白袴は乙の受手
甲の受手、叉黒襦

(圖　一　第)

Battling Two Opponents Using Spear, Sword & Jujutsu #1
Illustration 2

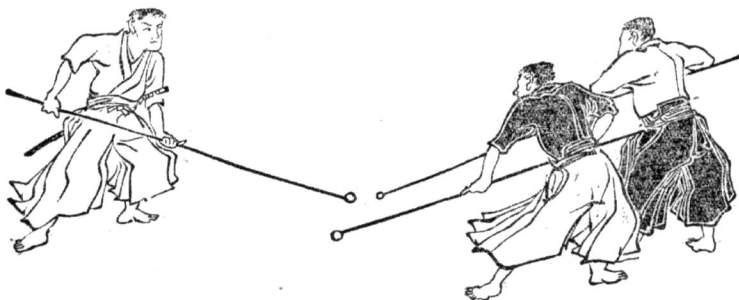

出せるを
槍を繰り
んざし、
手を突か
へて、使
穂先を揃
人が槍の
乙受手二
ごとく甲
第三圖の
次には此
曰ふなり
らば圖と
き伏せた
かけ、突
と掛撃を
開々開く
れも開く
なり、こ
ひたる所
て、見合

(圖　二　第)

Battling Two Opponents Using Spear, Sword & Jujutsu #1
Illustration 3

三十二　　劔鎗柔術二人捕

使手は防ぎて右へ押ゆるなり、押ゆるとは、押へて落し、又拂ひ除くるに用ゐるなり、突くうちにも之は、使手の面を突かむとするなり、受手は何れも押さへられて、退きて復たきて復た使手の胴

（第　三　圖）

Battling Two Opponents Using Spear, Sword & Jujutsu #1
Illustration 4

三十三　　劔鎗柔術二人捕

を突かむこして繰り出すを、使手は逆に下より受けて、槍の柄を刎ね上げ、此下の圖のごとく近よりて甲受の左の脇を、左脇を中て、悶絶させ、乙受は又、使手の面を突かんと槍を繰り出す押さへ再び面を突かんと繰出すよりすり出しを受け使手は槍を、第五圖のごとく、落さる因て直ちに、第六圖のごとく刀を拔きて向ひ、受手の槍に已たり合ふ、

（第　四　圖）

212

Battling Two Opponents Using Spear, Sword & Jujutsu #1
Illustration 5

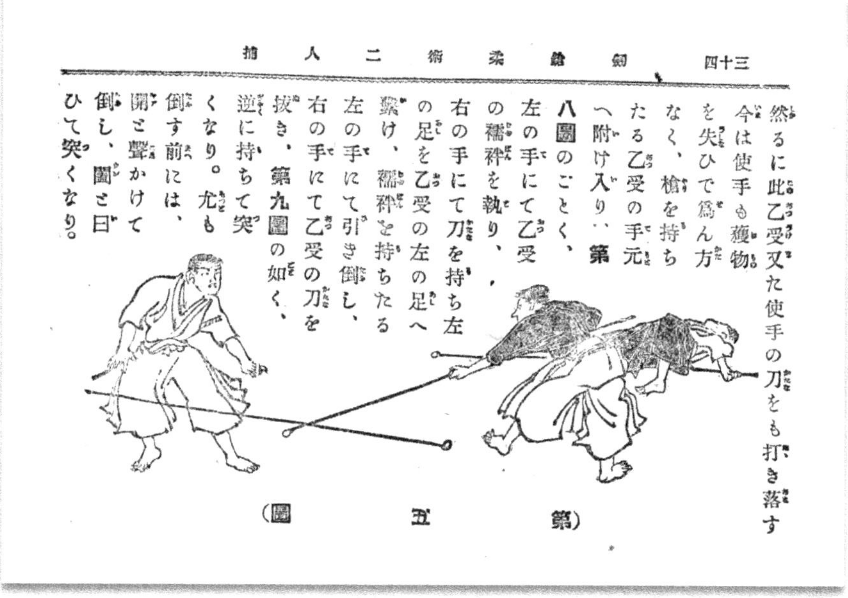

捕　人　二　術　柔　鎗　劍　　　四十三

然るに此乙受又た使手の刀をも打き落す
今は使手も獲物を失ひで爲ん方なく、槍を持ちたる乙受の手元へ附け入り、第
八圖のごとく、左の手にて乙受の襦袢を執り、右の手にて刀を持ち左の足を乙受の左の足へ蹴け、襦袢を持ちたる左の手にて引き倒し、右の手にて乙受の刀を逆に持ちて突く、第九圖の如く、抜き、右の手にて乙受の刀を逆に持ちて突くなり。尤も倒す前には、開き聲かけて倒し、圖る曰ひて突くなり。

（第　　五　　圖）

Battling Two Opponents Using Spear, Sword & Jujutsu #1
Illustration 6

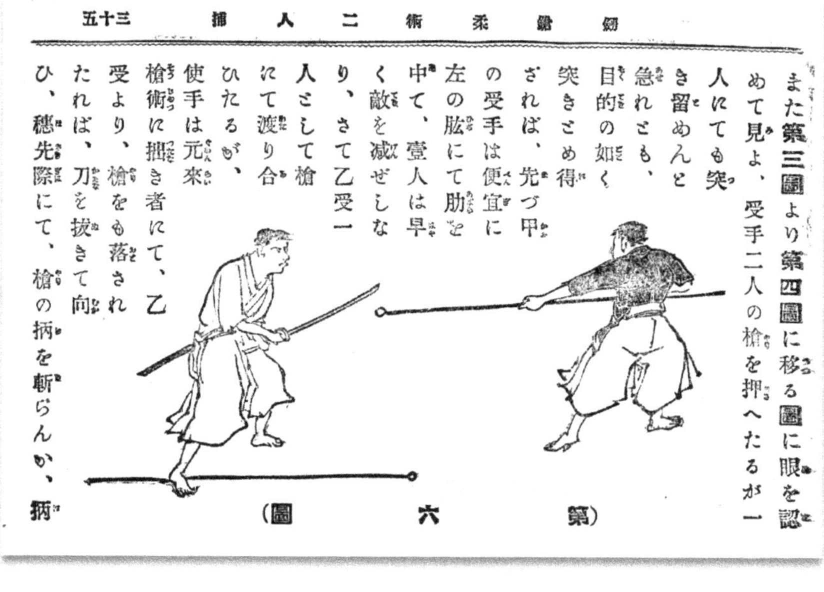

五十三　　捕　人　二　術　柔　鎗　劍

また第三圖より第四圖に移る圖に眼を認めて見よ、受手二人の槍を押へたるが一
人にても突き留めんと急れさも、目的の如く突きさめ得ざれば、先づ中の受手は便宜に左の脇にて肋を中て、壹人は早く敵を減ぜしなり、さて乙受一人さして槍にて渡り合ひたるが、使手は元來にて槍術に掴き者にて、乙受より、槍をも落されたれば、刀を拔きて向ひ、穗先際にて、槍の柄を斬らんか、柄

（第　　六　　圖）

Battling Two Opponents Using Spear, Sword & Jujutsu #1
Illustration 7

（第　七　圖）

Battling Two Opponents Using Spear, Sword & Jujutsu #1
Illustrations 8 & 9

（第　八　圖）

（第　九　圖）

● *Ken-So Jujutsu Futari Tori: Dai-Ichi Kata*
Battling Two Opponents Using Spear, Sword & Jujutsu #1

The sword techniques are from Sekiguchi Ryu[28] and the spear techniques are from Oshima Ryu.[29]

---

[28] The Sekiguchi School was founded by Sekiguchi Yaroku Uemon Ujimune 関口弥六右衛門氏心(1597~1670.) Sekiguchi studied Iai (sword drawing,) Kumiuchi (Jujutsu) and Chinese Kenpo under Miura Yoji Uemon. Sekiguchi wrote in *My Thoughts on the New Way of the Heart Yawara (Jujutsu)*柔新心流自序
「余蚤歳より斯の術に志あり。独限師承無し」
Set your mind to training this art diligently from a young age.
Train by yourself, you do not need a teacher.

[29] The Oshima School was founded by Oshima Yoshitsuna 大島吉綱(1588~ 1657.) It uses the Su-yari, straight spear, The spear used in this school is quite long at 1 Jo 8 Shaku 5 Sun, about 3.6 meters. The illustration below sketches the parts of the spear and gives the dimentions of the various parts.
From an 1854 document titled *A Catalogue of Oshima School Kuden*
大島当流槍術総目録箇条口伝之事

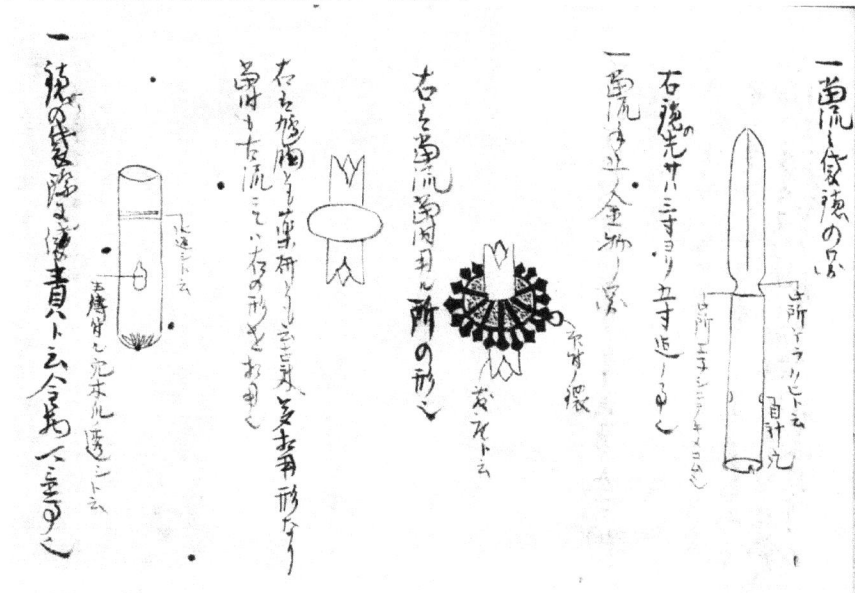

Battling Two Opponents Using Spear, Sword & Jujutsu #1

Illustration 1

The first illustration shows how you should position yourself for the initial bout of respect. When bowing the tip of your spear should always be facing to the left. As before you are shown wearing a white shirt and a white Hakama. The Ko-Uke is wearing a white shirt and black Hakama and the Otsu-Uke is wearing a black shirt and white Hakama.

Battling Two Opponents Using Spear, Sword & Jujutsu #1

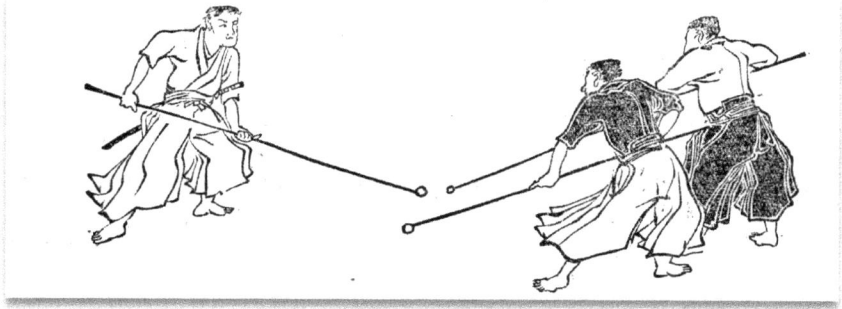

Illustration 2

As the second illustration shows, everyone stands and the spearfight will begin. Your right hand should be about 3 Sun, 9 centimeters, from the Ishizuki, the "attached rock" or weighted end of the spear. This is the proper way to hold a spear.

It's important that you do not hold the spear with your left hand on the Ishizuki. In addition, when you are attacking with your spear, you are not simply stabbing straight ahead, instead you are using Suri-komi, thrusting up from below. This is an important point to remember.

As the second illustration shows after bowing you stand. Your attackers are standing side by side attacking you with spear thrusts. Your plan is to defend against their thrusts. Note carefully how everyone is positioned in this illustration.

Battling Two Opponents Using Spear, Sword & Jujutsu #1

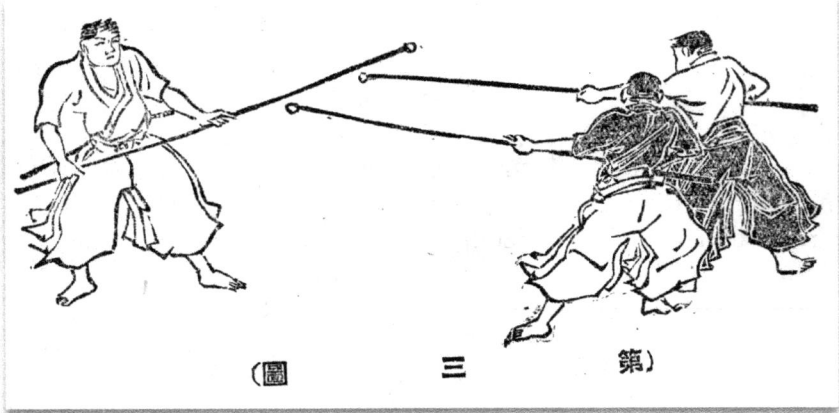

Illustration 3

When attacking, advance with your spear while shouting *Yaa! Yaa! Yaa! Yaa!* Yaa! If you succeed in striking your opponent and taking him down then you shout *Un!*

As the third illustration shows both attackers have lined up their spear points and are attacking you with repeated thrusts, stabbing their spears forward and then pulling them back. They then immediately stab forward again. You defend with Osae-yuru, which means shoving the attacking spear down and to the right. You also use your spear in a Harai, or sweeping action. The attackers continue to thrust towards your face and their combined attacks are forcing you back.

Battling Two Opponents Using Spear, Sword & Jujutsu #1

Illustration 4

Suddenly the Ko-Uke stops trying to stab your face and instead attacks your abdomen. You counter this by knocking his spear upward from below, forcing the shaft of his spear up into the air. Then, as shown in the fourth illustration, you move in and strike the Ko-Uke in the ribs with your left elbow knocking him unconscious.

Battling Two Opponents Using Spear, Sword & Jujutsu #1

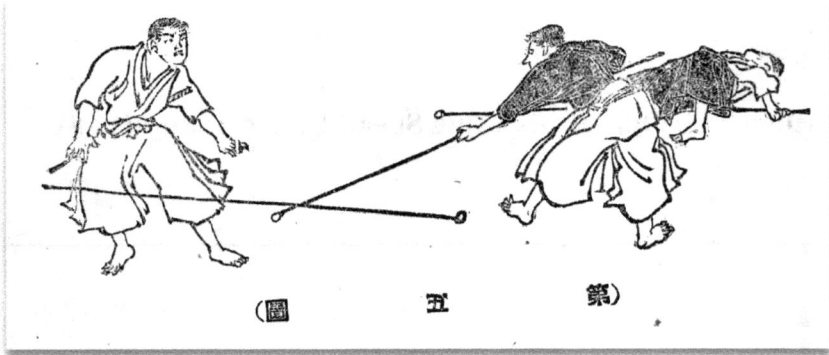

Illustration 5

The Otsu-Uke continues to advance stabbing at your face with his spear, pressuring you. You force one of his spear thrusts down however he stabs at your face again. Eventually, as shown in Illustration 5, he knocks your spear out of your hand.

Illustration 6

You respond as shown in Illustration six by drawing your Katana and joining combat, which is now sword against spear.

Battling Two Opponents Using Spear, Sword & Jujutsu #1

Illustration 7

However, the attacker also knocks the Katana from your hand and now you are like prey before the hunter, with no escape in sight. You take the only action you can and charge forward to the area known as Temoto, where his hands hold the spear.

Battling Two Opponents Using Spear, Sword & Jujutsu #1

Illustration 8

As the eighth illustration shows, having moved in close to the attacker's hands, you then seize his shirt with your left hand and seize the handle of his Katana with your right hand. Hook your left foot around the attacker's right foot. Use your left hand to shove him down as you draw his sword with your right hand.

Battling Two Opponents Using Spear, Sword & Jujutsu #1

Illustration 9

As the ninth illustration shows you stab him with the sword held in a reverse grip. Before you throw him down you should shout *Yaa!* and shout *Un!* as you stab him.

Illustration 3

Illustration 4

Be sure to carefully observe the transitions between illustrations three and four. You are trying to suppress the attacks of two opponents at the same time. In the course of this duel, you're hoping to stop one attacker and then rush in. Once you have stopped the Ko-Uke's attack, you take him out with a clever left elbow to the ribs on his left side. With this strike, you have quickly reduced the number of attackers by one. Now it is you and the Otsu-Uke.

Unfortunately, you are not a particularly skilled spear fighter. Your opponent succeeds in knocking your spear out of your hands and onto the ground. You draw your sword and face him. It is possible to eliminate the danger by cutting the shaft of the spear behind the spearhead. However, as the attacker is thrusting forward and then immediately yanking his spear back, it's not possible to make such a cut.

| *Illustration 8* | *Illustration 9* |

You are also not particularly adept at sword fighting, and soon your opponent has knocked your sword from your hands. You are now in a desperate situation that requires you take extreme action. Seizing the shaft of his spear you slide your hands up it until you are close enough to use your Jujutsu, your only remaining weapon.

Once you are close enough, seize his shirt, steal his sword, shove him down and stab him. This technique shows how the spear and the sword are used, however it primarily a Jujutsu technique. Jujutsu is considered the mother and father of the six martial arts[30], and the foundation on which martial skill is built.

If you only train with the sword or with the spear and ignore Jujutsu, you would be in trouble in the situation described above. While your opponents are skilled in the spear and the sword they are insufficiently trained in Jujutsu. For those seeking to become experts at martial arts, you need to train extensively in all weapons. When studying this technique, note all the transitions. I encourage all my readers to carefully observe how the technique progresses from one illustration to the next.

---

[30] The "Six Martial Arts" are: bow, horse, sword, spear, cannon and gun. Jujutsu is the base from which the others developed.

◉ *Ken-So Jujutsu Futari Tori: Dai-Ichi Kata*
Battling Two Opponents Using Spear, Sword & Jujutsu #2
Illustration 1

捕　人　二　術　柔　鎗　劔　八十三

◎劔槍柔術二人捕　第三形

礼式より此處に及ぶまでは前の如し、さて此初めは第一圖のごとく乙なる受手白襷黒襷白襷の者より、白襷黒襷白襷の使手は槍にて突く面を目がけて槍にて突くを使手は拂ひて腕腹を突き又、第二圖のごとく白襷黒襷羽の甲の受手、使手の面に突きかゝるを使手は薬ばやくすり落す、

（第　一　圖）

Illustration 2

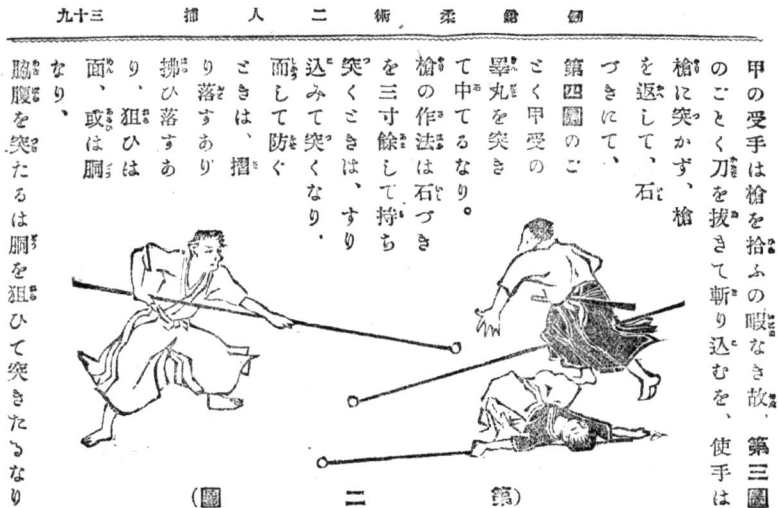

九十三　捕　人　二　術　柔　鎗　劔

甲の受手は槍を拾ふの暇なき故、第三圖のごとく刀を抜きて斬り込むを、使手は槍に突かず、槍を返して、石づきにて、第四圖のごとく甲受のごとく甲受の眉丸を突きて中てるなり。槍の作法は石づきを三寸餘して持ち突くさきは、すり込みて突くなり。而して防ぐさきは、攔り落すあり、狙ひは面、或は胴なり。挑ひ落すあり、狙ひは面、或は胴なり、脇腹を突たるは胴を狙ひて突きたるなり

（第　二　圖）

Illustration 3

槍を落されて、刀を拔
きて斬り込むには、
穂先を斬り落すか
柄を手繰りて、
手元へ斬り込
むかするなり
此形にて使手
が槍を返して
石づきにて受
きたるは斬り
込み來る都合
にて斯くせし
なり、
突き得らるゝ
ものを、強ちち
に畧丸を中てたる
にあらず、
通常に穂先にて突
くならば、面或は
胴を突くなれども

（第　三　圖）

Illustration 4

石づきにて突くこなれば、急所なる畧
丸を突くなり、さて、槍の突き方、刀の
使ひ方、柔
術の捕り方
何れも眞の
試合を識者
は側らに在
りて寫生し
たるものなれば、文
を讀みて意を取り、
圖を見て眞を知るべ
し、手つき、足
つき、體の樣子
實に目のあたり
に見るさ思ひて
見るべし、順序は寛
に肝要なり、捕り始
め、試合の始より順
序を遠へず、要を忘
れず、たびたび形を、相手を求めて習ひ
贊るべし。

（第　四　圖）

● *Ken-So Jujutsu Futari Tori: Dai-Ichi Kata*
Battling Two Opponents Using Spear, Sword & Jujutsu #2

Illustration 1

This technique begins the same way as the previous one with a mutual bow of respect.

As the first illustration shows the Otsu-Uke, who is wearing a black shirt and a white Hakama, is stabbing at your face. You, who are wearing a white shirt and a white Hakama, sweep his spear away and stab him in his left side.

Battling Two Opponents Using Spear, Sword & Jujutsu #2

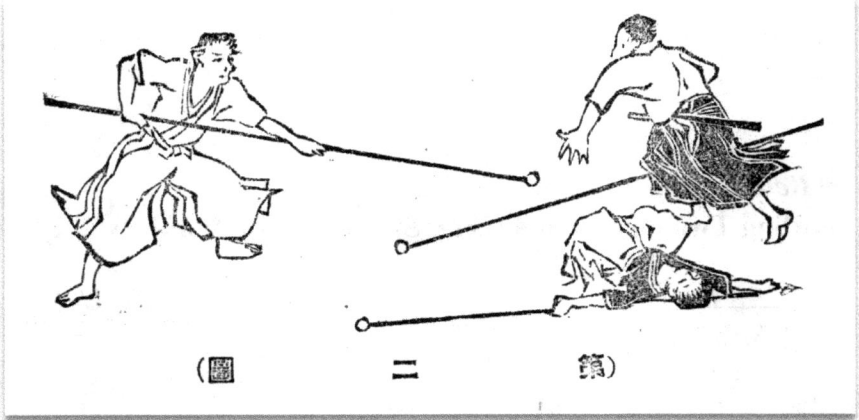

Illustration 2

Next, as the second illustration shows, the Ko-Uke, wearing a white shirt and black Hakama, stabs to your face with his spear. You respond by rapidly blocking this and sliding the shaft of your spear along his spear, forcing him to drop it.

Illustration 3

Your attacker does not have any time to pick up his spear so, as shown in the third illustration, he draws his sword and attacks.

Illustration 4

You respond, not by stabbing him, but by striking with the Ishizuki, weighted back end of your spear. As shown in the 4th illustration you strike him in the groin. The rules for handling the spear dictate that your right hand is 3 Sun, 9 centimeters, from the Ishizuki. When striking to the groin you are sweeping up from below with the end of your spear.

Other ways to defend when using the spear are Suri Otoshi, Slide and Drop, as well as Harai Otoshi, Sweep and Drop. When attacking, you aim for the face or abdomen. When you read the instruction "stab in the side" this means that you should aim for the abdomen.

When your attacker draws his sword and tries to cut you, he is aiming to slice the spear tip off your spear or slide his sword along the shaft of your spear up to your hands and cut. In this technique you are reversing your spear and striking the attacker in the groin with the Ishizuki, weighted end. The reason is because you feel this is the best way to respond to this attack. If your strike is accurate it doesn't have to be particularly strong.

When attacking with your spear you are directing your spear point at the face or the body, however when using the Ishizuki, you are aiming for a vital point like the groin.

When making sketches for this book the artist watched actual training. He watched how to attack with the spear, how the sword is moved and how Jujutsu is done. So, as you read the words I have written, look at the pictures and as you consider their meaning. Pay close attention to how the hands are positioned, how the feet are positioned and how the bodies of the combatants are depicted.

The order of action in these techniques is also very important. Make sure before you begin training, or begin a duel, you do not mistake the correct order. I recommend that you frequently practice these techniques with a partner.

明治三十九年六月十日發行
明治三十九年五月十五日印刷

不許複製

發賣元 叉間精華堂
大阪市心齋橋筋安堂寺町西入
（電話東一三六三番）

印刷者 菅田淳吉
大阪東區谷町大手前南入東側

發行者 叉間安次郎
大阪府區安堂寺橋通四丁目
二丁三十一番屋敷

著作者 久松定基
大阪府區安堂寺橋通四丁目

Published June 10th of Meiji 39 (1906)
Author:
Hisamatsu Sadamoto

www.ingramcontent.com/pod-product-compliance
Lightning Source LLC
Chambersburg PA
CBHW072125270326
41931CB00010B/1679